The Rohingya Crisis

A People Facing Extinction

Muhammad Abdul Bari

The Rohingya Crisis. A People Facing Extinction

First published in England by

Kube Publishing Ltd
Markfield Conference Centre
Ratby Lane Markfield Leicestershire
LE67 9SY United Kingdom

Tel: +44 (0) 1530 249230 Fax: +44 (0) 1530 249656

Website: www.kubepublishing.com Email: info@kubepublishing.com

Cataloguing-in-Publication Data is available from the British Library

ISBN 978-1-84774-124-0 Paperback
ISBN 978-1-84774-125-7 ebook
All Author proceeds from the sale of this book will go to the education of
Rohingya children, wherever they are.

Map and Image credits

Map 1 Shutterstock; Map 2 Wikimedia – CIA World Factbook, Public
Domain; Map 3 Wikimedia – Rohingya people in Rakhine (Arakan) State in
Myanmar; Map 4 ERCC Portal – European Commission; Map 5 Shwe Gas
Movement – Shwe.org; Image 1 Shutterstock; Image 2 Shutterstock

Cover image: Joel Carillet, iStock
Cover Design: S4Carlisle Publishing Services
Typesetting: S4Carlisle Publishing Services

Printed by: IMAK ofset, Turkey

Dedication

This book is dedicated to all people who have suffered from ethnic cleansing and genocide around the world.

Endorsements

Muhammad Abdul Bari's book *The Rohingya Crisis* provides a superb historical analysis of why Rohingya Muslims have been subject to decades of discrimination and exclusion. His extremely informative history on the persecution that the Rohingya have faced will undoubtedly help build awareness and understanding of the plight of the Rohingya population.

Well-sourced and accessible, this excellent book should be read by anyone wanting to understand the unbearable suffering currently afflicting the Rohingya.

Rushanara Ali, *MP for Bethnal Green and Bow*
Co-Chair, All Party Parliamentary Group for Democracy in Burma

We should all feel shame and anger of this terrible betrayal of the Rohingya people. This carefully written and eloquent short book by Muhammad Abdul Bari is carefully documented and records facts in a sober way. He makes clear that there is no question that what has occurred is a genocide.

Peter Oborne, *Columnist for the Daily Mail and Middle East Eye*

For anyone who wants a concise and readable explanation of the situation of the Rohingya, this is the book. The August 2017 Burmese military offensive which drove around 700,000 Rohingya into Bangladesh did not come out of the blue. It came after the systematic increase of repression and human rights violations against the Rohingya Muslim minority by the Burmese government and military. This book details the history and provides the context to help understand how and why this crisis happened, including the failure of the international community to protect one of the world's most persecuted minorities.

Mark Farmaner, *Director, Burma Campaign UK*

Dr Muhammad Abdul Bari's book about the plight of the Rohingya is both timely and significant. I congratulate him for bringing to the fore the scale and barbarity of the sheer pain and suffering inflicted on a people for so long. As someone who has witnessed genocide and massacres in my beloved Bosnia not long ago at the hands of the

Serbs, we really do feel and understand the suffering of the Rohingya Muslims. Like in Bosnia, what is striking in Myanmar is that the Rohingya have been, and continue to, suffer in silence without any credible international response. The feelings of isolation, helplessness and the lack of action from neighbours and those who boast freedom, human rights and justice, is the most difficult to accept.

The Serbian crime against Muslims in Bosnia was the worst in Europe since World War II, leaving a dark stain on Europe's human rights record, but the unending persecution of the Rohingya is a new world low which will affect generations to come. This book, I hope, will serve as an alarm bell to remind us all that: "In the end, we will remember not the words of our enemies, but the silence of our friends." (Martin Luther King)

Dr Mustafa Cerić, *Former Grand Mufti of Bosnia and Herzegovina*

Muhammad Abdul Bari has written a book that had to be written. While the world looks away, genocide is being committed by the Myanmar authorities against the Rohingya Muslims. The plans to erase the Rohingya and any memory of them cannot succeed. This urgent book bears witness to the oppression of the Rohingya so that there are no excuses: "that we did not know". This book is a reminder that no justice for the Rohingya diminishes us all.

S. Sayyid, *Professor of Rhetoric and Decolonial Thought, University of Leeds*

In camps from Calais to Cox's Bazar, there are hundreds upon thousands of people who have been forced by violence, disaster and persecution, to flee their homes. On this often perilous journey, they lose a part of themselves, who they are, along the way. We often say 'Never Again', but every day there continues to be systematic persecution of the Rohingya in Myanmar, while in the refugee camps, children are facing trafficking and malnutrition. The Government of Bangladesh and British humanitarian agencies are responding to challenges on the ground, but much more needs to be done to ensure that those responsible for genocide are brought to justice.

With this short book by Dr Bari, there is now an easily accessible record of the historical background and the unfolding humanitarian tragedy. It includes an eloquent personal perspective of the responsibility that now rests on the shoulders of the UN, the

Bangladesh Government and other key players. He urges that any repatriation of refugees to Myanmar must ensure their full citizenship status, freedom of movement and removal of the discriminatory laws of the past. This book is an effort to keep the Rohingya issue alive.

Dr Rosena Allin-Khan, *MP for Tooting, UK*

Contents

Maps and Images

Acknowledgements

In the aftermath of the Myanmar military's latest vicious operation against the Rohingya, volumes of information from various media sources and individuals close to the conflict continued to pour onto my desk whilst writing this monograph. I am grateful to all those, in Bangladesh and elsewhere, who have been conscientiously monitoring events on the savage eviction of a people from their homeland in Rakhine State to Bangladesh and regularly sending me reports, books, articles, news links and pictures.

I am indebted to Rumman Ahmed, Peter Oborne and Dr Jamil Sherif for their meticulous observations and thoughtful ideas as well as their inspiring comments on the first draft. My thanks go to Mark Farmaner, Dr Thomas MacManus, Kyaw Win, Nick Ryan and Salman Farsi for their contribution and ideas in the final draft of the manuscript.

Time is of the essence in such a volatile situation and I am grateful to Kube Publishing for being able to get the book edited, designed and printed in such a short time.

I am grateful to our youngest son, Adib, who in spite of heavy pressure in his job and studying towards a professional qualification, was able to do the editing of the subsequent drafts. My gratitude to Sayeda, my wife, and other members of the family for their encouragement knows no bound. Acknowledging all the others by name is going to be an impossible task.

This short book has been written with the main aim of helping the long-persecuted Rohingya people in their struggle for survival and justice. It is imperative for morally upright people anywhere in the world to stand with the Rohingya until they all are repatriated to their homeland in Myanmar with safety and full citizenship rights. All proceeds from this book will go to charity, especially toward the education of Rohingya children.

I seek forgiveness from the Almighty God for any mistake and shortcoming in this book.

Foreword

Future generations will look back at the genocide of the Rohingya people and feel disbelief that it was ever allowed to happen. Yet all the warning signs were there well in advance.

The Rohingya have suffered systemic discrimination for many years. They were denied rights to public services; they suffered organised violence; they were herded into camps and denied all civil rights, including the right to vote. Indeed, the Myanmar government has refused to accept the humanity of the Rohingya people while allowing Buddhist monks and others to spread lies and whip up hate against them.

After a number of terrible warning episodes, genocidal violence finally erupted in late August last year. We know that more than 10,000 Rohingyas have been murdered and more than 688,000 have fled across the border to Bangladesh. Countless women have been raped. This horror continues and one fears for the remaining Rohingya inside Rakhine State. Their situation gets worse and worse.

Yet the international community has done nothing. Aung San Suu Kyi remains in power, and remains the proud possessor of a Nobel Peace Prize. There is no talk even of targeted sanctions against her commanding general, Min Aung Hlaing. This dreadful sequence of events has been gravely underplayed in the western media.

Hence the need for this carefully written and eloquent short book by Muhammad Abdul Bari. His work is carefully documented and records facts in a sober way. He makes clear that there is no question that what has occurred is genocide.

Early last year, I visited the memorial in Bosnia to the 7,000 Bosnian Muslims who were systematically murdered by the Serbs in 1995. Even then it seemed to me quite bewildering that this could have taken place in Europe as the United Nations sat idly by. Yet it has happened again in Myanmar, and once again the United Nations have done nothing. Once again, the world has failed to lift a finger.

We should all feel shame and anger at this terrible betrayal of the Rohingya people. Meanwhile, we can feel gratitude to Muhammad Abdul Bari who has performed a public service in writing and publishing this tragic record.

Peter Oborne: Columnist for the *Daily Mail* and *Middle East Eye*.

Preface

The long suffering of the Rohingya people in Arakan (now Rakhine) in Burma (now Myanmar) and the shamefully ineffective global actions taken to help them are symptoms of our morally broken world. The Rohingya situation worsened significantly after Burma's independence in 1948. However, since the military coup led by General Ne Win in 1962, persecution on them has multiplied and they have faced violence, arbitrary arrest and detention, extortion, restriction of movement, discrimination in education and employment, confiscation of property, forced labour and other abuse. Ruled by a Revolutionary Council and a one-party system (*Burma Socialist Programme Party*), the country went through rampant ethnic strife, with some groups on the south, east and north borders involved in a long-running civil war. Burma was known for its poverty and systematic human rights violations for decades. As the Rohingya people were declared 'aliens', organised and aggressive persecution on them by the military junta included Burmanization of the Rakhine administration, banning their socio-cultural organisations and even denying their identity as the 'Rohingya'; the regime even ended the Rohingya language programmes being broadcast from Rangoon (now Yangon) Radio.

Two big operations to evict them (in 1978 and 1991–92) were so vicious within a short period of time that hundreds of thousands crossed the river Naf that separates Myanmar and Bangladesh and arrived at Bangladesh's Cox's Bazar district. With the help of the United Nations (UN), Burma and Bangladesh reached agreements for Rohingya repatriation; many refugees returned, some migrated to other countries and others remained in Bangladesh's refugee camps. But the Burmese government was not sincere in its commitment to this agreement and violent discrimination against the Rohingya continued unabated. The situation has worsened since 2012 when more than 100,000 refugees were virtually encamped in IDP (internally displaced person) camps.

However, the Rohingya plight reached epic proportions in August 2017. The world watched with horror the scorched-earth policy undertaken by the Myanmar military, aided by ultra-nationalist Buddhist groups. The exodus of frightened Rohingya people from Rakhine State to Bangladesh in the first few weeks after 25 August 2017 was of biblical proportions and many places in their ancestral homeland became almost Rohingya-free. This was called a 'textbook example of ethnic cleansing' by the UN and drew widespread condemnation, but global inertia as well as power politics seem to be hindering or denying a just solution to this latest human tragedy. This has shown the heartless face of a powerful group's inhumanity toward a weak 'other' in our morally skewed world.

On the basis of eyewitness accounts from charities, human rights bodies and global media establishments, as well as from satellite pictures of indiscriminate burnings of Rohingya homes, history will decide whether this cruel treatment of a minority community constitutes crimes against humanity or genocide. This vividly reminds the world community of the plight of Bosniak people and Rwandans in our lifetime, only a quarter century ago. Once again, the post-war 'never again' promises made by the civilised world after the horrors of the Second World War are shown to be hollow and embarrassing rhetoric.

The Rohingya have a long and rich history in Burma. There is no exact official figure, but according to government around 4 per cent of Myanmar's 53 million people are Muslims and the Rohingya are a significant group; however, Myanmar Muslims claim the proportion is much higher. While the Rohingya have been living there for centuries, they have been denied citizenship rights by the post-independence Myanmar military authorities that refused to recognise them as one of the country's 135 ethnic groups. The Rohingya language has some resemblance to Bengali, with a strikingly similar dialect to that of Bangladesh's Chittagong district, which borders with Myanmar. The dialect is a mixture of Arabic, Persian, Bengali, Arakanese, Portuguese and other south Asian languages.

I grew up in a village in central Bangladesh where there was a Hindu minority, but no Buddhist or other communities; one of my best school friends was a Hindu from the lower caste. When I attended Chittagong University in the south east of Bangladesh in the early 1970s to do my undergraduate degree in Physics, I fell in love with the people, the rich heritage, as well as the landscape of Chittagong. I could easily count one Chakma Buddhist[1] and one

---

1   The world Chakma population is estimated to be over half a million. The majority, approximately 300,000, live in the Chittagong Hill Tracts of Bangladesh. They have their own language, customs and culture, and profess Theravada Buddhism. For more details, see The Editors, 'Chakma, People' (Encyclopædia Britannica, 11 July 2002). Available at: https://www.britannica.com/topic/Chakma (accessed on 31 January 2018).

Christian (of Portuguese extraction) as close friends. My Chakma friend was a polite and sociable young man who was always smiling; he was loved by everyone for his amiable personality. By that time I was aware of the dynamics among the three major religions of South Asia – Hinduism, Buddhism and Islam. As someone interested in history, I learned about the founder of Buddhism, Siddhārtha Gautama, who brought a unique spiritual tradition to ancient India over two millennia ago and suggested that the root cause of human suffering is 'ignorance'. Whether his followers in Myanmar are driven by ignorance or hatred towards their neighbouring Rohingya people is a matter that needs investigation.

I travelled widely across the Chittagong region, including Cox's Bazar and Chittagong Hill Tracts. With the help of my close Chittagonian friends, I eagerly learned to communicate in their dialect; I found it difficult to speak but I could understand most of it. The dialect has been imprinted on me and even after four decades I can understand most of what the Rohingya refugees have been saying in their own dialect. But, embarrassingly, I did not have much knowledge about the Rohingya across the Cox's Bazar border, in Arakan, at that time. However, when I was posted as a Bangladesh Air Force officer to Chittagong Air Base in early 1982 I visited various places there during the weekends and on holidays. By that time, the first batch of Rohingya people had already arrived at Cox's Bazar as refugees in 1978 and many had also returned. I learned more about the Rohingya during that period, so when the recent wave of brutally violated Rohingya people started crossing the Naf River and arriving at the muddy refugee camps in August 2017, with their horrific recollections, I could immediately connect with them.

Arakan was, for a long period in history, the centre of a rich literary and cultural heritage of Muslims in the south eastern part of the South Asian subcontinent. This gradually declined with the general Muslim degeneration, exacerbated by the weakening of the Mughal Empire and ultimate take over by British colonialists. During my time in Chittagong University there were a number of prominent academics of Chittagonian origin, such as Professor Muhammad Yunus in the Economics department (who was later awarded the 2006 Nobel Peace Prize) and Professor Dr Abdul Karim in the History department (who became Vice-Chancellor of the university in 1975). Dr Abdul Karim's authoritative history book in English, *The Rohingyas: A short account of their history and culture*, published in 1997, is highly rated in Bangladesh.

According to the UN, the number of those who fled from Rakhine State since 25 August 2017 currently stands at 688,000,[2] and still there are reports of new arrivals. This has raised the overall number of Rohingya refugees in Bangladesh to over one million (there were about 400,000 of them from previous exoduses). On 14 December 2017, Médecins Sans Frontières (MSF), gave a conservative figure of at least 6,700 Rohingya deaths, including at least 730 children under the age of five, between August and September 2017. In spite of its densely populated land, Bangladesh has shown an exemplary humanitarian face – thanks to the generosity of ordinary people and the government's agreement to allow them in. Unless the world community, coordinated through the UN, quickly comes up with a long-lasting pragmatic and just solution to repatriate all the Rohingya to their homes in Myanmar with safety and full citizenship rights, this could open up a new humanitarian crisis, as well as political and security challenges in southeast Asia.

The inhuman treatment of the Rohingya – being uprooted from their land, exiled, expelled, burnt, beaten up, destroyed, devastated, raped, and shot to death – by Myanmar's military machine and Buddhist extremists is another ugly face of violence to fellow human beings. It is an irony that followers of a world religion, Buddhism, which has its 'fundamental goal as peace and not harming any living thing', have perversely turned their hatred and guns on the most impoverished, weak and passive community in their midst – the Rohingya. In a short book of this size we cannot go into details as to why this is happening, but in a post-9/11 anti-Muslim climate the Rohingya people's religious identity might have exacerbated their plight. This may also be the reason why Rohingya sufferings of this scale have not attracted enough angst and anger from world leaders who have the ability to take action and help the beleaguered Rohingya people.

I have been involved in charity and humanitarian works since the mid-1990s, and as someone of Bengali ethnic origin, I feel it is my responsibility to learn more about the Rohingya and come to their help in some way. As many people have been serving the Rohingya in those areas quite effectively, I thought it best to write about their plight

---

2   Office of the High Commissioner, 'End of mission Statement by Special Rapporteur on the situation of human rights in Myanmar' (OHCHR, 1 February 2018). Available at: http://www.ohchr.org/EN/NewsEvents/Pages/DisplayNews.aspx?NewsID=22619&LangID=E (accessed on 2 February 2018).

and encourage others towards more practical action. This short book about the horrible Rohingya suffering on such a large scale and in such a short time (I am aware other ethnic groups have also suffered under Myanmar's brutal military rule) is aimed at creating awareness of Rohingya's history and their current predicament amongst, primarily, the diaspora Rohingya and the diaspora Bangladeshi people; this will hopefully be useful to all friends of the Rohingya and other upright people in their persistent efforts to raise global awareness in order to find a just and long-term solution. The Rohingya catastrophe is wholly man-made and needs global determination in convincing the Myanmar authority to adhere to our core and universal human value of 'live and let live'. This, to my knowledge, fully conforms to Buddhist humanitarianism and basic justice.

Introduction

Before the ink of the Advisory Commission on Rakhine State's final report[1] (*Towards a peaceful, fair and prosperous future for the people of Rakhine*) was dry, on 25 August 2017 Myanmar's military and police forces, supported by the Rakhine Buddhist chauvinists, launched a scorched-earth policy on the minority Rohingya Muslim population in Rakhine. The Commission was set up by the Myanmar government itself and was led by former UN Secretary-General Kofi Annan.

The severity and speed of anti-Rohingya operations were unparalleled in recent history. From that fateful day onward, hundreds of thousands of Rohingya men, women and children have been forced to leave their homes under appalling brutality. Hungry, destitute, and ashen-faced they poured towards the Bangladesh border. Although Bangladesh had already previously given shelter to about 400,000 Rohingya in various refugee camps in southern Chittagong after three crackdowns in 1978, 1991–92 and the most recently in October 2016, this massive influx caught the country, as well as the world community, by surprise. Bangladesh had to open its borders to save fellow human beings from annihilation. Myanmar gave a flimsy justification of their barbaric retaliation, saying it was because of ARSA[2] (Arakan Rohingya Salvation Army) attacks on some of its military and police posts that killed a dozen officers. It

---

1   Advisory Commission on Rakhine State, *Towards a Peaceful, Fair and Prosperous Future for the People of Rakhine: Final Report of the Advisory Commission on Rakhine State* (Geneva: Kofi Annan Foundation, 2017). Available at: http://www.rakhinecommission.org/app/uploads/2017/08/FinalReport_Eng.pdf (accessed 30 January 2018). In August 2016, former UN Secretary-General Kofi Annan was invited to head the Advisory Commission on Rakhine State. The complete report was published a year later, on 25 August 2017, and accepted by the government of Myanmar. Violence erupted on the same day, culminating in the forced displacement of over 650,000 Rohingyas who took shelter in neighbouring Bangladesh.

2   ARSA is a small, low-intensity insurgent group previously known as the Harakah al-Yaqin (meaning Faith Movement) that sprung up in 2016 because of continued persecution of an otherwise peaceful and passive Rohingya people. For decades the Rohingya had shown little inclination towards armed struggle. ARSA is known to be comprised of around 200 people and is very poorly armed. In their first operation in 2016 they killed nine police officers, and in August 2017 a dozen army and police officers were killed by them. In a statement released on

is difficult to discover why the ARSA took this suicidal step, but the disproportionality of the government's response and its banning of the world media in Rakhine whilst inexcusable atrocities took place has shocked the civilised world. It is also pertinent to note that in all the months after the August attacks, the international media have not reported even a single ARSA attack in Rakhine!

The emergence of a ragtag ARSA, with no or little support from the people, has been primarily due to decades of inhumane treatment of the Rohingya. Myanmar has been marred by prolonged insurgency from various ethnic groups since its independence due to the lack of democracy and a ruthless military dictatorship. Even in Rakhine State the ethnic Rakhine Arakan Army[3] (AA), founded in 2009 and closely allied with the Kachin Independence Army (KIA), has been 'fighting for self-determination'. As recently as 30 November 2017, an AA spokesperson accused the Myanmar Army of launching a large-scale assault on them suggesting that 'the ongoing clashes between the Myanmar Army and the Arakan Army are likely to intensify in the coming days'.[4] Insurgency by other groups has been persistent, organised and strong, but none of them have faced the wrath of the military rulers on this scale in such a short time frame. One explanation is that although consisting of a tiny number of disenchanted Rohingya Muslims, the ARSA appears to represent 'the other'; while the AA, with a higher capability of harming the Myanmar army and establishment, is seen as one consisting of their 'own people'. Racism and religious bigotry rules in modern Myanmar!

On 8 September 2017, the veteran South African Nobel Laureate Archbishop Desmond Tutu took an unprecedented step by criticising his fellow Nobel Laureate Daw Aung San Suu Kyi, Myanmar's *de facto* civilian leader or State Counsellor, saying: 'If the political price of your ascension to the highest office in Myanmar is your silence,

---

14 September 2017, ARSA denied any link with foreign or transnational jihadist networks.

3   Oliver Holmes, 'Myanmar army clashes with ethnic Rakhine rebels' (*The Guardian*, 8 January 2016). Available at: https://www.theguardian.com/world/2016/jan/08/myanmar-army-clashes-ethnic-rakhine-rebels-killed (accessed 30 January 2018).

4   Htet Naing Zaw, 'AA, Myanmar Army Clashes Likely to Intensify: Arakan Army Spokesman' (*The Irrawaddy*, 30 November 2017). Available at: https://www.irrawaddy.com/news/burma/aa-myanmar-army-clashes-likely-intensify-arakan-army-spokesman.html (accessed 30 January 2018).

the price is surely too steep'.[5] Tibet's Dalai Lama echoed global criticism of attacks on the Rohingya ethnic minority, saying; 'Buddha would have helped the Rohingya Muslims who are fleeing violence in Buddhist-majority Burma'.[6] Sadly, the Dalai Lama has been a lone voice in the world Buddhist community. Although Buddhism and violence has been known to be an oxymoron, no other senior Buddhist leader or leader of any Buddhist majority country such as Japan, Thailand, Sri Lanka, or Bhutan has been heard condemning this twenty-first century inhuman massacre of a small minority by the Myanmar regime. Religion talks about compassion and politics talks about rights, but this has been dismally absent from Buddhists and politicians alike in Myanmar and other Buddhist majority countries.

It is noticeable that no prominent western leader has been heard criticising Buddhism for this 'Buddhist' crime, whereas a Muslim or Muslim group is not spared from incrimination in a similar situation. No one called upon Buddhists to take the blame and call out 'not in our name', as Muslims are regularly urged to do. The duplicity is stark!

The UN was established after the Second World War to avoid human tragedy and to make the world a better place; but many now are raising questions about its effectiveness, especially since its failures in Cambodia, Bosnia and Rwanda. Human Rights Watch (HRW) and Amnesty International accused the UN Security Council of ignoring the plight of the Rohingya and demanded that it hold an open meeting to end the violence. By 11 September 2017, the number of Rohingya people fleeing from Myanmar had risen to 300,000 and the head of the UN High Commission for Human Rights, Zeid Ra'ad al-Hussein, accused the Myanmar government of a 'textbook example of ethnic cleansing'.[7] 'The operation [...] is clearly disproportionate and without regard for basic principles of international law,' Mr Hussein

5   Naaman Zhou and Michael Safi, 'Desmond Tutu condemns Aung San Suu Kyi: "Silence is too high a price"' (*The Guardian*, 8 September 2017). Available at: https://www.theguardian.com/world/2017/sep/08/desmond-tutu-condemns-aung-san-suu-kyi-price-of-your-silence-is-too-steep (accessed 30 January 2018).

6   Will Worley, 'Dalai Lama: Buddha would have helped Burma's Rohingya Muslims' (*The Independent*, 11 September 2017). Available at: http://www.independent.co.uk/news/world/asia/dalai-lama-rohingya-muslims-buddha-burma-help-myanmar-buddhist-india-tibet-a7941101.html (accessed 30 January 2018).

7   Roland Oliphant and Nicola Smith, 'UN human rights chief slams Burma for "textbook ethnic cleansing", as Dalai Lama says Buddha would help Rohingya' (*TheTelegraph*, 11 September 2017). Available at: http://www.telegraph.co.uk/news/

said. Subsequently, in early December, he said that it amounted to almost genocide. According to refugees and human rights groups, 'the Burmese military and local vigilantes are systematically targeting civilians in a campaign of terror characterised by house burnings, mass shootings, beheadings, and gang rape'.

The UN Security Council condemned the violence and Secretary-General António Guterres said on 13 September 2017 that ethnic cleansing could lead to a 'catastrophic humanitarian situation for the Rohingya Muslim minority'.[8] But in the absence of a willingness to help the Rohingya from global powers such as China (which has a huge influence on Myanmar) the voices of UN leadership are ineffective. In the cost–benefit analysis, the Rohingya must be seen by some world powers as expendable as opposed to keeping up a good relationship with the Myanmar military!

In an unprecedented step, on 13 September thirteen Nobel laureates and twenty-three eminent global citizens came together and wrote to the UN Security Council[9] for an intervention to end the human crisis in Rakhine.

As this short book was being written, over 688,000 Rohingya have taken shelter in Bangladesh; they carry stories of the horrors they have endured with them, only a fraction of which are being reported in the mainstream media. With large numbers of Rohingya already living in Bangladeshi camps, the number of displaced men, women and children has now risen to over one million. Most parts of northern Rakhine, the heartland of the Rohingya people for centuries, has been turned Rohingya-free. Bangladesh, the world's most densely populated developing country, is trying its best to cope with financial help from some Muslim and other countries, yet the UN is struggling to tackle yet another global catastrophe. Surprisingly, in the current amoral world of nationalism-driven politics, even the UN itself is

---

2017/09/11/dalai-lama-says-buddha-would-help-burmas-rohingya-muslims-pressure/ (accessed on 30 January 2018).

8   Edith Lederer, 'UN chief calls for end to "ethnic cleansing" of Rohingya Muslims as Security Council condemns violence' (*The Independent*, 13 September 2017). Available at: http://www.independent.co.uk/news/world/asia/rohingya-ethnic-cleansing-genocide-latest-aung-san-suu-kyi-refugees-burma-myanmar-un-bangladesh-a7945806.html (accessed on 30 January 2018).

9   News Desk, 'Amartya Sen signs open letter seeking UN intervention to Rohingya crisis' (bdnews24.com, 19 September 2017). Available at: https://bdnews24.com/bangladesh/2017/09/19/amartya-sen-signs-open-letter-seeking-un-intervention-to-rohingya-crisis (accessed on 31 January 2018).

failing. Its July 2017 assessment revealing desperate hunger among the persecuted Rohingya population was shelved at Myanmar's request.[10] Hunger remains hunger, whether a report on it is published or not, and people often die from hunger and malnourishment.

Charities across the world, including Britain's Disasters Emergency Committee (DEC), have made emergency appeals[11] for humanitarian assistance for the Rohingya in Bangladesh. Initially confused and hesitant, Bangladesh opened its doors to malnourished and frightened Rohingyas thanks to its citizen's sympathy for the refugees coming across the border; a public outpouring that turned the Prime Minister's heart. Bangladesh has earned the world's genuine praise[12] for this generosity. But it does not want to bear the burden of the Rohingya for long. For reasons not exactly clear, some renowned British charities were ordered to stop aid to the Rohingya in the refugee camps in Cox's Bazar.[13]

Many compare the situation in Rakhine state with that of the Bosniak Muslims[14] who faced genocide in the early 1990s from the Serbs. An 18-month long research study found evidence that the persecution of the stateless Rohingya – including corralling them into ghettos, sporadic massacres and restrictions on movements – amounted to a long term strategy by Myanmar's government to isolate, weaken and eliminate the group. The report concluded that the 'dehumanisation and stigmatisation' techniques used against

---

10   Oliver Holmes, 'UN report on Rohingya hunger is shelved at Myanmar's request' (*The Guardian*, 17 October 2017). Available at: https://www.theguardian. com/world/2017/oct/17/un-report-on-rohingya-hunger-is-shelved-at-myanmars-request (accessed on 31 January 2018).

11   Disasters Emergency Committee, 'Emergency Appeal for the Rohingya people'. Available at: https://www.dec.org.uk/?gclid=CjwKEAjwsNfOBRCWl _HevZSJ2i0SJABiE2qWBkoZ9Jdy_xTkmPwHv3M7ghXYg8FOQdVjtk4kG faf3hoCIW3w_wcB (accessed on 31 January 2018).

12   News Desk, 'Commonwealth Secy Gen praises Bangladesh response to Rohingyas refugees' (*The Daily Star*, 17 September 2017). Available at: http:// www.thedailystar.net/world/rohingya-crisis/commonwealth-general-secretary-patricia-scotland-praises-bangladesh-response-to-rohingyas-1463506 (accessed on 31 January 2018).

13   BBC News, 'Bangladesh orders charities to stop aid to Rohingyas' (BBC News, 2 August 2012). Available at: http://www.bbc.co.uk/news/world-asia-19092131 (accessed on 31 January 2018).

14   Yasmin Qureshi, '20 years after Srebrenica, the Rohingya are the Bosnians of today' (*New Statesman*, 11 July 2015). Available at: https://www. newstatesman.com/politics/2015/07/20-years-after-srebrenica-rohingya-are-bosnians-today (accessed on 31 January 2018).

Rohingyas warrant comparison with Germany in the 1930s and Rwanda in the early 1990s.[15] Justice (that has to be colour-blind) is not yet in sight for the Rohingya.

Myanmar has blocked most international agencies, including the UN, from parts of northern Rakhine State. But atrocities by the security forces were being recorded with satellite images and the Red Cross has had greater access than anybody else. Elhadj As Sy, the head of the world's largest humanitarian network, the International Federation of Red Cross and Red Crescent Societies (IFRC), has described the humanitarian crisis affecting Myanmar's Rohingya Muslims as unprecedented and said the world was failing in its response.[16] Even in November 2017, 'thousands of Rohingya continue to arrive in Bangladesh each day' said Sy.

The Rohingya minority has often been called the most persecuted minority in the world,[17] unable to claim citizenship in a country they have been living in for generations. Famous British journalist Peter Oborne visited the Bangladesh–Myanmar border in November 2017 to witness the tragedy and gave a harrowing description of burning dead bodies, small children being thrown into fires or rivers, and women being raped and killed. According to him, a 'genocide is taking place under the nose of feted Nobel Peace Prize winner Aung San Suu Kyi'.[18] Oborne lamented that it is no exaggeration to say that 'this is one of the most heinous crimes of the 21st century', and accused world leaders of doing nothing to stop it. The world community

---

15   Lindsay Murdoch, '"Dehumanisation and stigmatisation" of Rohingya Muslims based on Nazism' (*The Sydney Morning Herald*, 29 October 2015). Available at: http://www.smh.com.au/world/dehumanisation-and-stigmatisation-of-rohingya-muslims-based-on-nazi-germany-report-20151029-gklsmg.html (accessed on 31 January 2018).

16   Poppy McPherson, 'World failing Myanmar's Rohingya Muslims, top Red Cross official says' (*The Guardian*, 26 October 2017). Available at: https://www.theguardian.com/world/2017/oct/26/world-failing-myanmars-rohingya-muslims-top-red-cross-official-says (accessed on 31 January 2018).

17   News Desk, 'The Rohingyas: The most persecuted people on Earth?' (*The Economist*, 13 June 2015). Available at: https://www.economist.com/news/asia/21654124-myanmars-muslim-minority-have-been-attacked-impunity-stripped-vote-and-driven (accessed on 31 January 2018).

18   Peter Oborne, 'Slaughter of the innocents: Searing eye-witness accounts from the genocide taking place under the nose of feted Nobel Peace Prize Winner Aung San Suu Kyi' (*Daily Mail*, 5 November 2017). Available at: http://www.dailymail.co.uk/news/article-5052485/Slaughter-innocent-Rohingya-refugees-Myanmar.html (accessed on 31 January 2018).

had great hope in Suu Kyi, but she is now seen as 'part of the problem'.[19]

On 10 November 2017, in an open letter titled 'The Rohingya are facing genocide. We cannot be bystanders',[20] dozens of prominent individuals, including Salman Rushdie, expressed their horror on the Rohingya situation: 'The international response to the Rohingya crisis has fallen far short of what's needed. [...] The corporations that are competing for investment in Myanmar must speak up and divest, unless human rights are respected, or they too will be complicit in these horrendous acts [...] We cannot allow people to be slaughtered and burnt out of their homes, while the world watches.'

Myanmar has refused to allow the UN or outside organizations or journalists to conduct any independent investigation.[21] It has even published its own report and found no evidence of systemic violence against the Rohingya! But the torching of houses has been captured by satellite images, as reported by Amnesty International.[22]

Britain, with its historic links with Myanmar as the main colonial power and as a permanent member of the UN Security Council, has a huge moral and global responsibility to initiate some practical steps to resolve the Rohingya crisis. At the Lord Mayor's Banquet on 13 November 2017, Prime Minister Theresa May spoke about the 'desperate plight of Rohingyas – brought home to us again on our TV screens so graphically today, with heart-breaking images of young children emaciated and pleading for help'.[23] She vowed to play

---

19   Karen McVeigh, 'Aung San Suu Kyi complicit in Rohingya "ethnic cleansing" in Myanmar, MPs told' (*The Guardian*, 15 November 2017). Available at: https://www.theguardian.com/global-development/2017/nov/15/aung-san-suu-kyi-complicit-in-rohingya-ethnic-cleansing-in-myanmar-mps-told (accessed on 2 February 2018).

20   Salman Rushdie, Kiran Desai, Madhur Jaffrey, and others, 'The Rohingya are facing genocide. We cannot be bystanders' (*The Guardian*, 10 November 2017). Available at: https://www.theguardian.com/commentisfree/2017/nov/10/rohingya-genocide-ethnic-cleansing-never-again (accessed on 31 January 2018).

21   Sarah Gibbens, 'Myanmar's Rohingya Are in Crisis—What You Need to Know' (*National Geographic*, 29 September 2017). Available at: https://news.nationalgeographic.com/2017/09/rohingya-refugee-crisis-myanmar-burma-spd/ (accessed on 31 January 2018).

22   Amnesty International, 'Myanmar: Crimes against humanity terrorize and drive Rohingya out' (18 October 2017). Available at: https://www.amnesty.org/en/latest/news/2017/10/myanmar-new-evidence-of-systematic-campaign-to-terrorize-and-drive-rohingya-out/ (accessed on 31 January 2018).

23   Rt Hon Theresa May MP, 'PM speech to the Lord Mayor's Banquet 2017' (Prime Minister's Office, 13 November 2017). Available at: https://www.gov.uk/

a leading role in bringing the international community together 'to stop this appalling and inhuman destruction of the Rohingya people'. But so far, at the time of writing this book, no serious efforts have been initiated as her weakened government struggles with Brexit negotiations.

Towards the end of November 2017, the Trump administration in America changed its weak position on Myanmar. After visiting the country, Secretary of State Rex Tillerson said: 'it is clear that the situation in northern Rakhine State constitutes ethnic cleansing against the Rohingya'.[24] This might have put some pressure on Myanmar's military and civilian administration, but the world needs a concerted effort.

In spite of the UN calling this ethnic cleansing and a catastrophe, the Security Council remains ineffective on the impending disaster visited upon Myanmar's Rohingya people. The main reason, as usual, lies with the lack of unity amongst its permanent members. A narrow nationalistic and mercantile interest, devoid of moral compass, seeks to compete in Myanmar's increasingly open market and seems to be dictating the global powers' agenda. Unless the world community and public opinion exerts strong pressure on the Myanmar government through the UN, the Rohingya people may end up being homeless for a long period and pawns of global politics for decades to come.

International humanitarian and human rights groups have been consistently expressing their frustrations on the UN failure to find a dignified solution to the Rohingya crisis. However, towards the end of November 2017, the world suddenly came to know of a bilateral deal signed by Myanmar and Bangladesh in Myanmar's capital NayPyidaw to allow the return of Rohingya refugees in Bangladesh.[25] Very little was published and very little was expected of this. The wide cynicism was that this exercise was just for public consumption in Bangladesh. Since most Rohingya people had fled Rakhine for their lives, as many of their homes and villages were burned to the

---

government/speeches/pm-speech-to-the-lord-mayors-banquet-2017 (accessed on 31 January 2018).

24   Mark Landler, 'Myanmar's Crackdown on Rohingya Is Ethnic Cleansing, Tillerson Says' (*The New York Times*, 22 November 2017). Available at: https://www.nytimes.com/2017/11/22/us/politics/tillerson-myanmar-rohingya-ethnic-cleansing.html (accessed on 31 January 2018).

25   BBC News, 'Myanmar Rohingya crisis: Deal to allow return of Muslim refugees' (BBC News, 23 November 2017). Available at: http://www.bbc.co.uk/news/world-asia-42094060 (accessed on 31 January 2018).

ground, it is quite unlikely that they would ever be able to produce any credible documentary evidence to prove that they were former residents of Rakhine. The London-based Burma Human Rights Network (BHRN) called this bilateral deal 'deeply flawed'.[26] It urged that UNHCR should have a formal role in the return process, making sure Rohingya's 'rights, including citizenship and the right to self-identify on any government documents, are guaranteed'. As evicted Rohingya people have no possessions apart from their lives, repatriation should include material support to restart their life and a cast-iron guarantee of their security.

On 5 December 2017, Zeid Ra'ad al-Hussein, the UN human rights chief, addressed the Council session in Geneva saying a further act of genocide against Rohingya Muslims by state forces in Myanmar cannot be ruled out.[27] 'No Rohingya should be sent back unless there was sustained human rights monitoring on the ground', he suggested.

According to a conservative figure released by Médecins Sans Frontières on 14 December 2017, more than 6,700 Rohingya Muslims, including at least 730 children under the age of five, were killed between August and September:[28] 'The majority of the people killed (69%) were shot, while others were burned and beaten to death', the MSF reported. However, the Myanmar government is still in complete denial and claim to have killed only 400 'terrorists'. The Myanmar government's argument of 'rooting out Rohingya militants' simply does not wash; it has actually meant a horrific and well-planned 'rooting out the Rohingya'. Rohingya people are still fleeing from Myanmar, and those who do manage to reach Bangladesh relate harrowing stories that should shake and stir the conscience of the international community towards action.

In a resolution (adopted by a vote of 122 to 10 with 24 abstentions) on 23 December 2017, the UN General Assembly urged Myanmar

---

26   Press Release, 'Bilateral Agreement On Rohingya Repatriation Deeply Flawed' (Burma Human Rights Network, 30 November 2017). Available at: http://www.bhrn.org.uk/en/press-release/30-press-release-bilateral-agreement-on-rohingya-repatriation-deeply-flawed.html (accessed on 31 January 2018).

27   BBC News, 'Rohingya crisis: UN rights chief "cannot rule out genocide"' (BBC News, 5 December 2017). Available at: http://www.bbc.co.uk/news/world-asia-42234469 (accessed on 31 January 2018).

28   Poppy McPherson, '6,700 Rohingya Muslims killed in one month in Myanmar, MSF says' (*The Guardian*, 14 December 2017). Available at: https://www.theguardian.com/world/2017/dec/14/6700-rohingya-muslims-killed-in-attacks-in-myanmar-says-medecins-sans-frontieres (accessed on 31 January 2018).

to end its military campaign against the Rohingya and called for the appointment of a UN special envoy.[29] Unfortunately, China and Russia voted against the resolution and the Myanmar authorities, as usual, insisted the campaign was only aimed at 'rooting out Rohingya militants'. However, the resolution called on the government 'to allow access for aid workers, ensure the return of all refugees and grant full citizenship rights to the Rohingya'.

---

29   Agence France-Presse, 'China and Russia oppose UN resolution on Rohingya' (*The Guardian*, 24 December 2017). Available at: https://www.theguardian.com/world/2017/dec/24/china-russia-oppose-un-resolution-myanmar-rohingya-muslims (accessed on 31 January 2018).

1 Origins of the Arakanese Muslims[1]

Myanmar, Bangladesh and the Indian Ocean

---

1   Abdul Karim, *The Rohingyas: a short account of their history and culture* (Chittagong: Arakan Historical Society, 1997).

Arakan[2] is a coastal region of the south Asian subcontinent, with the Bay of Bengal to its west, Bangladesh and India to its north and Burma proper (isolated by the Arakan Mountains, also called Arakan Yoma) to its east. It is a long narrow strip of land along the eastern seaboard of the Bay of Bengal. Arakan stretches from the Naf River estuary on the border of Bangladesh's Chittagong district. It is about 400 miles long from north to south and about 90 miles wide at its broadest. The Arakan coast has several sizable offshore islands and one-tenth of Arakan's generally hilly land is cultivable.

In order to deny the Rohingya their rights and citizenship, Burmese administrations have been trying to prove they were immigrants brought by the British colonial rule in the nineteenth and twentieth centuries. But history has established that in fact Muslims arrived in what was then the independent kingdom of Arakan (now Rakhine) as long ago as in the eighth century,[3] around the time when the Vikings first visited Britain in 789 CE. They were originally seafarers and traders from the Middle East, and renowned Bangladeshi historian Dr Abdul Karim suggests there were four phases of Muslim presence in Burma.

The first phase

As far back as the early period of Islam, highly-spirited Arab traders were exploring the world, with trading activities from the Red Sea to far flung areas such as the Chinese coast and Arakan within Burma (now the state of Myanmar). It is difficult to ascertain exactly when Arabs arrived at Arakan, but they established contact during eighth to tenth centuries. Some came to Chittagong in Bengal and others to the Ayeyarwady (or Irrawaddy) River Delta in Arakan. Maungdaw, in northern Arakan, became one of their favourite destinations. All this happened prior to the establishment of the first Burmese empire in 1055 CE by the pagan King Anawrahta Minsaw.[4]

During the reign of the Burmese king Mahato Tsandaya (788–810 CE) several Arab ships were wrecked off the coast of the

---

2   The Editors, 'Arakan State, Myanmar' (Encyclopædia Britannica, 20 July 2002). Available at: https://www.britannica.com/place/Arakan (accessed on 31 January 2018).

3   'The Rohingyas' (*The Economist*, 13 June 2015).

4   The Editors, 'Anawrahta, King of Myanmar' (Encyclopædia Britannica, 20 July 1998). Available at: https://www.britannica.com/biography/Anawrahta (accessed on 31 January 2018).

Rambi Islands and sailors were rescued from the shore. They were taken to the king who allotted a piece of land for them, where they were allowed to settle. As a trading people, these early Arab settlers were inspired by Islam's message of universalism; some indigenous people might have accepted Islam in this early period.

The second phase

In the early fifteenth century there were huge political upheavals in Arakan. The Arakanese king, Min Saw-Mun, was defeated by the Burmese King in 1406 CE and expelled from his kingdom; he took refuge in Bengal which was then ruled by Ghiyasuddin Azam Shah. But Bengal itself witnessed several palace intrigues, groups and fighting at that time. Eventually, Min Saw-Mun regained his territory with the help of Jalal-ud-din Mohamed Shah, the Sultan of Bengal, and returned to the kingdom after about a quarter of a century. His stay in Bengal gave him a great deal of knowledge about Bengali, Arabic and Persian languages and literature. During his reinstatement, a large contingent of Muslims from Bengal (several thousand) entered Arakan in 1430 CE. They were mainly soldiers and administrators who were needed to help the reinstated king regain his throne, but many of them stayed behind after their mission was complete. Min Saw-Mun naturally made some agreements with his benefactor, the Sultan of Bengal, before he was restored; one was bearing the cost of the expedition. He used Muslim titles with the court emblem inscribed with the Islamic *Kalimah* (declaration of faith) and used Persian as the court language. He transferred the Arakan capital from Launggyet to the city of Mrauk-U, near the eastern coast of the Bay of Bengal, which became a vibrant city with a diverse range of people establishing mosques, temples, shrines, seminaries and libraries.

In effect, from 1430 to 1531 Arakan remained a protectorate of the Bengal Sultanate. According to historians, Arakan kings were Buddhists and there is no proof that any of them accepted Islam, but their voluntary practice of adopting Muslim names continued for more than two hundred years. Min Saw-Mun himself adopted the name of Sulaiman Shah or Sawmun Shah and ruled Arakan until his death in 1434 CE. Historians have argued as to why Arakanese kings, especially in the sixteenth and seventeenth centuries, adopted Muslim names even though they were Buddhists and independent rulers. The likely explanation is Muslims were probably seen as culturally more sophisticated during that period.

3

During the fifteenth and sixteenth centuries, various specialists and professional people, as well as some prominent individuals including renowned Bengali Muslim poets, came to Arakan. Some of them settled in the capital Mrauk-U, often known as Mrohaung or Roshang. This further enlivened the capital city with religious, social and cultural activities. Arab traders also frequented Arakan until the sixteenth century.

In the seventeenth century, some renowned Bengali Muslim poets wrote of their impression that the capital city of Roshang (Mrohaung or Mrauk-U) thronged with Muslims in the courts as well as in religious, social and cultural assemblies. Then there were Muslim artisans, craftsmen and traders, as well as men connected with the mint and other state establishments.

The third phase

This phase began with the arrival of the Europeans in the seventeenth century, with their superior vessels and better merchandise; at that time, the Arabs began to lose their edge in the eastern trade. This group of settlers included both Muslims and Hindus, who were kidnapped from the coastal areas of Bengal by Portuguese pirates[5] and Arakanese Maghs[6] and sold to slavery. The Portuguese pirates had a particular racial hatred and religious aversion to Moors,[7] and by extension any Muslim, probably because they were ruled by Arabs some centuries earlier. During this period, the Arakanese Magh kings employed the Portuguese to loot and plunder the coastal districts of Bengal; the Maghs joined them in these criminal attacks. These raids became widespread and continued for a long time. Ordinary people in the coastal Bengal areas used to live in fear, and the term *Moger Mulluk*, meaning an anarchic state, has since been used in the Bengali language because of the dreaded piracy of that period. I came across this term from the elders in my childhood.

---

5   When the Bengali Sultanate became weakened in the sixteenth and seventeenth centuries, Portuguese-Arakanese piracy increased against Mughal Bengal and ravaged the Arakan coast.

6   The term is used for the Arakanese or Rakhine people. They joined hands with Portuguese pirates and were involved in the slave business in the seventeenth century.

7   The term refers primarily to Muslims of North Africa, the Iberian Peninsula, Sicily, and Malta during the Middle Ages. It also refers to Arabs.

Some of the slaves captured by the Portuguese pirates were sold to priests who converted them to Christianity. The Maghs mostly used their captives for manual labour, such as tilling the soil, cutting trees and felling. Thousands of Bengali captives (Muslims and Hindus) were made to settle in Arakan, thus increasing the Muslim and Indian population there. Some of them were released when the Mughals took over Chittagong.

The fourth phase

This began in the middle of the seventeenth century, when power politics at the heart of the Mughal Empire in India forced one of Aurangzeb's brothers, Shah Shuja, to take shelter in Arakan. In addition to his family, there were around 1,000 Muslims in his entourage. The Arakanese king gave them asylum, but once he proposed to marry a daughter of Shah Shuja, the relationship between them turned sour. Ultimately, Shah Shuja was murdered with his family by order of the king. However, those in Shah Shuja's entourage stayed behind and along with the existing Muslims contributed towards building a pluralist Arakan.

2 Arakan's Thriving Legacy

The Rohingya Muslim legacy in Arakan is rich. This is their ancestral homeland, where Muslim rule and influence lasted for centuries, particularly during the glorious period of Mrauk-U from early 1430 to 1784 that saw a thriving age of power and prosperity with multi-ethnic and multi-religious people living together in relative peace and harmony. With a hybrid Buddhist-Islamic court, it successfully fused traditions from Persia and India with the Buddhist world in the east. There were opportunities for all: Muslim Qazi courts were set up throughout the kingdom; Persian and Bengali languages were not only patronised but used as the court languages; coins and medallions inscribed with the Muslim *Kalimah* (declaration of faith) in Persian and Arabic script were often minted; Muslim trade and business also flourished, as they were also the main providers of agriculture.

The Arakanese poet, Syed Alaol[1] (1607–73), was the most prominent of all poets in Roshang. Born in the Faridpur district, he was the son of a Bengali Minister, but he ended up in Arakan as a captive of Portuguese pirates while travelling by boat with his father. His father died a martyr, but Syed Alaol was sold in Arakan and appointed a horseman in the Arakan army. Alaol was a learned man with a literary knowledge of Bengali, Arabic, Persian and Sanskrit languages. He had a natural disposition to poetry, and as his reputation as a scholar and poet spread, high-ranking officials, including Prime Minister Magan Thakur, patronised him in many ways. Alaol wrote

---

1   See, 'Aloal' (Wikipedia, 13 January 2014). Available at: https://en.wikipedia.org/wiki/Alaol (accessed on 31 January 2018).

a number of famous books and is considered to be one of the most prolific medieval Bengali Arakan poets. His most well-known work is *Padmavati,* which depicted the story of Padmavati (a Sinhalese princess) and the queen of Chittor (a city in Rajasthan, India). He wrote on the unique nature of human diversity in the then Arakan and his poems drew upon his deep spirituality. Since most of his poems combined emotion with intellect, he has been called the *Pandit Kobi* (Wise Poet) of medieval Bengali literature.

While writing on the Rohingya history of Arakan, Dr Abdul Karim also mentions the immense Muslim contribution and their huge influence in politics, culture, literature and other walks of life during the sixteenth and seventeenth centuries. Sadly space means that I can only offer a glimpse of this here.

Historical evidence shows that there were at least three Prime Ministers (Magan Thakur, Sayyid Musa and Nabaraj Majlis), three Defence Ministers (Burhanuddin, Ashraf Khan and Bara Thakur) and two Ministers (Sayyid Muhammad and Srimanta Sulaiman) who were Muslims[2] and contributed greatly to Arakan's rich history. In addition, many Muslims were appointed as Judges (called *qazi* or *qadi* in Arabic) following the examples of the Bengal Sultanate. One of the judges, Daulat Qazi, was also a renowned poet and Sufi; he was born in Bengal's Chittagong district and started writing a book at the request of Defence Minister Ashraf Khan, who himself was of Sufi inclination. Daulat Qazi[3] died before he could finish his work and it was later completed by Alaol. There were famous religious figures from Arakanese Muslims as well, such as Sayyid Masum Shah and his son Sayyid Mustafa, and many Muslims also joined the Army.

However, this thriving period was coming to its end by the second half of eighteenth century, when the nearby Bengal Sultanate was taken over by the British East India Company in 1757 due to the treachery of its army commander and the archetypal deception of the Company; Chittagong fell in 1760 and in the aftermath, there were border skirmishes between Arakan and Chittagong. Amidst factional fighting and political turmoil in Arakan, the Burmese king Bodawpaya (1745–1819) conquered Arakan in 1785 and annexed it as a Burmese province.

---

2   Karim, *The Rohingyas.*
3   See, 'Daulat Qazi' (Wikipedia, 8 July 2005). Available at: https://en.wikipedia.org/wiki/Daulat_Qazi (accessed on 31 January 2018).

But Arakan power was weakening. In the first Anglo-Burmese war of 1825, Arakan lost and the British occupier soon built the city of Akyab (now Sittwe, the capital of Rakhine State), at the confluence of the Kalandan river as Arakan's new capital. Arakan's new English civil ruler, Thomas Campbell Robertson, quickly realised the economic potential of Arakan's fertile but fallow land; however, he found the menfolk in matriarchal Burma to be lazy. In a report to the then Governor-General of India he requested farmers from Bengal, especially Chittagong, to cultivate the Arakanese land. According to the report, the Muslim population of Arakan was 30,000 – 30 per cent of the total population. With the new arrival of Muslims (plus some Hindus) from Chittagong, the number increased further. The Chittagonian farmers were successful in their trade and some moved into other professions such as business.

According to a 1911 census, in the Akyab district alone the number of Muslims was 178,647, which was 33 per cent of the total population, a significant increase in the overall population. Arakan Muslims were not monolithic; although the Rohingya during that period were the majority (80 per cent), the rest were from other backgrounds. The post-independence Arakan in Burma accommodated the Rohingya reasonably well, but after the military takeover in 1962, the Burmese government deliberately distorted the picture to make it seem as if the Rohingya population was small. During the 1978 eviction of over 250,000 Rohingya to Bangladesh, it was known that the Rohingya population was over a million. In 1981, the government declared Arakanese Muslims as foreigners and in 1992, a human rights group reported in their bulletins that there were 1.4 million Rohingya people in Arakan.

3 British Rule and Post-Colonial Rohingya

Burma was ruled by the British from 1826 to 1948. The occupation took place in three phases: Arakan fell first in 1826, then southern Burma in 1852 – in the second Anglo-Burmese War – and the rest in 1885 in the third Anglo-Burmese War. Until 1937, the country was ruled from British India. British colonial enterprise was known for extracting maximum profit from the colonies and the British are known to have gained mastery by using a 'divide and rule' policy to keep colonial people under control. Burma's majority population, the Buddhists, saw the British favouring minority ethnic groups such as the Christian Karens and Muslim Rohingya. Also, after the British decision to bring a good number of economic migrants to Arakan from the Indian subcontinent, albeit for the fact that there was a shortage of skilled labour among the existing population, Burmese Buddhists developed a particular dislike for the British as well as envy and intolerance towards the Indians.

As a result of the arrival of these Bengalis and other Indians, Muslims and Hindus, the Arakan population rose considerably; however, the overall population also increased. The feelings of nationalist Buddhists were rising and they derogatively started calling the Indian people (Muslims and others) *Kala*.[1] Because of this arrival of

---

1   See, 'Persecution of Muslims in Myanmar' (Wikipedia, 20 October 2017). Available at: https://en.wikipedia.org/wiki/Persecution_of_Muslims_in_Myanmar

Muslims from Bengal during the British colonial period, the Myanmar establishment has always tried to 'prove' that all Rohingya are Bengali immigrants. This is a deliberate twisting of historical reality in order to inflict persecution on the Rohingya and get rid of them.

The global economic crisis in the 1930s affected Arakan a great deal. Buddhist farmers had to borrow money from Indians, but they could not repay their debts. As a result of this default, Bengalis and Indians became major landlords and rose to prominence in the government as well as in the economic sector; nationalist Buddhists felt further marginalised. During Buddhist uprisings against British colonialism in the early 1930s, they targeted other ethnic and religious minority groups such as the Rohingya, and the anti-colonial riots of 1938 were also aimed at the Rohingya community. 'The seeds for deep divisions in the country along religious lines had already been sown'.[2]

Japan's occupation of Burma in 1942 during the Second World War heightened Arakan's internal division as the region became the front line of conflict between Japan and Britain. Buddhists put their lot behind the Japanese, and as the British were desperately looking for allies the Rohingya gave them much-needed support. The British formed a guerrilla army called the 'V' force that recruited and armed Arakanese Muslims, The 'V' force operated 'along the whole front line between the British and Japanese armies'.[3] During Japanese occupation, the frequency and intensity of attacks on the Rohingya rose considerably. The Japanese occupation army itself carried out attacks on the Rohingya in retaliation for their pro-British stance, and the availability of arms to both the Buddhist and the Rohingya camps brought lawlessness resulting in the breakdown of Arakan's civil administration. The consequences were dire for both communities; Buddhists and the Rohingya were becoming increasingly segregated. Many Rohingya fled to northern Arakan, some even to Bengal, from the Japanese-controlled Buddhist-majority in southern Arakan. Once in a relatively safe area, the Rohingya also started conducting tit-for-tat retaliatory attacks against Buddhists in Muslim-dominated

---

(accessed on 31 January 2018). See also, Engy Abdelkader, 'The history of the persecution of Myanmar's Rohingya' (The Conversation, 21 September 2017). Available at: http://theconversation.com/the-history-of-the-persecution-of-myanmars-rohingya-84040 (accessed on 31 January 2018).

2   Azeem Ibrahim, *The Rohingyas: Inside Myanmar's Hidden Genocide* (Oxford: Oxford University Press, 2016), p. 27.

3   Clive J. Christie, *A Modern History of Southeast Asia: Decolonization, Nationalism and Separatism* (London: Tauris Academic Studies, 1996), p. 165.

north Arakan, causing Buddhists to flee to southern Arakan. Tens of thousands of people from the two communities lost their lives, villages were burnt and people were displaced. From 1942 until Britain pushed the Japanese out of Burma in 1945, 'Arakan experienced all the horrors that are the fate of any region trapped between two opposing armies'.[4]

Meanwhile, in India during the anti-British independence movement of the 1940s, Hindus and Muslims diverged from their goals; majority Muslims were gradually opting for a separate homeland in the name of Pakistan. As the Pakistan Movement was gaining momentum, some Rohingya organised a separatist movement to join Pakistan's eastern wing. Other Rohingya believed the British had promised them a Muslim National Area in northern Arakan in return for their support, but whatever the veracity of this claim this did not materialise once Japan was defeated. Hugely disappointed with the situation and because of a fear for their future, Rohingya leaders asked for direct support from Muhammad Ali Jinnah, the founder of Pakistan, to incorporate the Mayu region into East Pakistan. But the request was reportedly turned down by Jinnah[5] as he thought it would be seen as interference in Burmese matters.

At the time the British were leaving Burma, the country had a recognised border with the inhabitants from majority Burmese Buddhists, but also some non-Burmese ethnic people (such as the Rohingya, Karens and Shan) in the west, east and north. Some groups, like the Karens and Shan, initiated their long insurgency against Burmese rule. However, compared to many armed insurgencies by these groups and communists in post-independent Burma, separatism in Arakan was probably not as violent.

Many Burmese nationalists were driven by distrust for the ethnic populations who supported the British and wanted them side-lined. But General Aung San, who was the founder of the Burmese armed forces (known as Tatmadaw) and led Burma's independence from British rule, argued that the new free Burma should retain its secular nature and accommodate all who lived within Burmese border as equal citizens. But he was assassinated in 1947, six months before independence.

Amidst this state of chaos, Burma gained independence on 4 January 1948. The Rohingya immediately realised their precarious condition, as Buddhists were far more prominent in Arakan's

---

4   Ibid. p. 165.
5   Ibrahim, *The Rohingyas*, p. 27.

socio-economic and political life. The central government in Rangoon was struggling with post-independence chaos; a struggle from which arose three separatist trends in Arakan: the Buddhist nationalists, the Communists, and the Rohingya insurgency (some calling it a jihad). The Rohingya even gained control of a large part of northern Arakan. Some Rohingya leaders naively approached Burma's Constituent Assembly in Rangoon with a petition for Maungdaw and Buthidaung districts to join East Pakistan (now Bangladesh). This had a long term negative consequence on Rohingya loyalty to Burma.[6] With the military gradually becoming organised, the Rohingya insurgency was defeated in 1954.

Although they were not one of the named ethnicities that were given full nationality in the 1947 Constitution, the Rohingya were recognised as an indigenous ethnic group during the democratic government of the Prime Minister U Nu in the 1950s. They were represented in Parliament and government institutions and a radio station was established to broadcast programmes in the Rohingya dialect. The 1961 census indicated that the Mayu district, bordering the then East Pakistan, was 75 per cent Rohingya, a notable recognition.

But the situation dramatically worsened after the military coup in 1962. During the 1960s, under Ne Win's isolationist and chauvinistic government,[7] many South Asians were forced to leave Burma, particularly from the capital Rangoon. The government nationalised many enterprises of the white collar Burmese Indian community, which forced over 300,000 Indians to leave the country between 1962 and 1964. Its Westminster-style political system came to an end – with Rohingya's political and civil rights being trampled on. Since the late 1960s, the Rohingya have faced a new phase of violence, arbitrary arrest and detention, extortion, restriction of movement, discrimination in education and employment, confiscation of property, forced labour and other abuses.

The military junta's one-party system, the *Burma Socialist Programme Party*, did not waste time in closing the Rohingyas social and political institutions. Many private Rohingya businesses were taken over by the government, sapping their financial backbone. The country overall suffered widespread ethnic strife, and long-running brutal civil wars in some areas undermined Burma's progress. Burma

---

6   Ibid. p. 27.
7   The Editors, 'Yangon, Myanmar' (Encyclopædia Britannica, 20 July 1998). Available at: https://www.britannica.com/place/Yangon (accessed on 31 January).

became known for poverty and systemic human rights abuses. The junta cleverly used a mixture of Theravada Buddhism and Burmese nationalism to bolster its rule and started Burmanization of the Rakhine administration. Continued persecution of the Rohingya rendered them aliens in their own land. Their socio-cultural organisations were banned and even the Rohingya language broadcasts from Rangoon Radio station were ended.

Any knowledgeable person would be aware that the bouts of Rohingya violence or insurgency against the government in post-independence Burma were never a strategically coordinated or centrally-structured form of extremism or terrorism as we see today. Also, in terms of intensity, regularity and longevity, this cannot be compared with any of the well-funded and well-organised groups in the south, east and north of Myanmar that had previously waged war against the government. There has never been any survey of the Rohingya attitudes on extremism, but given the way they had been marginalised, as well as the nature of their passivity, any fair-minded observer would suggest that they have little or no connection with any of the violent groups that suddenly appeared in the name of Rohingya in Rakhine. The overwhelming proportion of the Rohingya had been living in extremely miserable conditions year after year.

As the 1947 Constitution did not formally recognise the Rohingya people as citizens, they could not become citizens in 1977 when the army launched a national drive to register citizens; they were once again left in total limbo. The major military operation to evict the Rohingya started on 6 February 1978. The campaign, known as Nagamin or Dragon King,[8] was so vicious that within a span of three months over 250,000 Rohingya refugees crossed the river Naf and arrived at Bangladesh's Cox's Bazar district. With the help of the UN, an agreement was reached between Burma and Bangladesh and some refugees returned to start a new life in Rakhine. However, the Burmese government's discrimination and violence against the Rohingya continued unabated and often became exceedingly disproportionate in terms of ferocity.

The 1982 Burma Citizenship Law created three categories of citizenship: *Citizenship*, *Associate Citizenship*, and *Naturalized Citizenship*. This excluded Rohingya from being citizens and made

---

8   See, 'Operation Dragon King' (Wikipedia, 19 November 2011). Available at: https://en.wikipedia.org/wiki/Operation_Dragon_King (accessed on 31 January 2018).

them a people without any rights, meaning they were declared stateless. The Rohingya could not own property or participate in political activities. The UN Special Rapporteur at the time called on the Burmese government to abolish the discriminatory requirements for citizenship. This did not happen and the Rohingya remained in a miserable limbo.

Initiated by students against Ne Win's dictatorship, nationwide pro-democracy political unrest (often known as the 8888 Uprising) shook Burma in 1988. The military inflicted heavy casualties on the protesters and retook power under General Saw Maung, who established the State Law and Order Restoration Council (SLORC). The new military junta changed the country's name to Myanmar in 1989 and held general elections[9] on 27 May 1990. Aung San Suu Kyi's National League for Democracy (NLD) won 392 of the 492 seats; but the junta refused to recognise the results. Another wave of persecution against the Rohingya in 1991–92 again drove over 250,000 refugees to Bangladesh's Cox's Bazar. The same exercise through the UN brought some of them back to Rakhine. But the situation was further worsening.

Political repression and economic misconduct for over four decades under military rule brought about another round of serious protests by students, political activists and Buddhist monks that started on 15 August 2007. Dubbed the Saffron Revolution, people defied 'the corrupt, inept, brutal generals who rule them, they took to the streets in their hundreds of thousands to demand democracy'.[10] This time Buddhist monks played a significant role.[11]

On 2–3 May 2008, a devastating storm known as cyclone Nargis caused more than 138,000 deaths and catastrophic destruction mainly in the densely populated Irrawaddy delta. This had a devastating impact on Myanmar:[12] an estimated 65 per cent of Myanmar's rice

---

9   See, 'Myanmar general election, 1990' (Wikipedia, 22 November 2015). Available at: https://en.wikipedia.org/wiki/Myanmar_general_election,_1990 (accessed on 31 January 2018).

10   News Desk, 'The saffron revolution' (*The Economist*, 27 September 2007). Available at: http://www.economist.com/node/9867036 (accessed on 31 January 2018).

11   See, 'Saffron Revolution in Burma' (Burma Campaign UK, 2007). Available at: http://burmacampaign.org.uk/about-burma/2007-uprising-in-burma/ (accessed on 31 January 2018).

12   Donald M. Seekins, 'The Social, Political and Humanitarian Impact of Burma's Cyclone Nargis' *The Asia-Pacific Journal*, vol. 6, no. 5 (May 2008). Available at: http://apjjf.org/-Donald-M.-Seekins/2763/article.html (accessed on 31 January 2018).

Myanmar and surrounding countries

fields and 95 per cent of the buildings in the delta region, inhabited partly by the Karens, were destroyed. The regime's legitimacy was further eroded because of its mishandling of the crisis; Myanmar had no choice but to open up slightly to the incoming international aid. The Junta organised a referendum in May 2008 that approved the new constitution and called a general election on 7 November 2010 in accordance with the constitution; this was boycotted[13] by Suu Kyi's National League for Democracy (NLD) and the Rohingya situation remained unchanged.

---

13   BBC News, 'Suu Kyi's NLD party to boycott Burma election' (BBC News, 29 March 2010). Available at: http://news.bbc.co.uk/1/hi/world/asia-pacific/8592365.stm (accessed on 31 January 2018).

The Annual Report (2011)[14] of the US Commission on International Religious Freedom stated:

> Muslims in Rakhine state, in the western coast, and particularly those of the Rohingya minority group, continued to experience the most severe forms of legal, economic, religious, educational, and social discrimination [...] The government has, in recent years, ordered the destructions of mosques, religious centers, and schools. During the reporting period, the Burmese government maintained a campaign to create 'Muslim Free Areas' in parts of Rakhine state.

For more than fifty years the Rohingya suffered from prejudice, discrimination and hatred under the military regime. As they were stripped of citizenship and then treated as stateless, they were subjected to stringent restrictions on freedom of movement and denied basic services such as access to medical care and education. All this rendered them a pariah people or outcasts in their own country, with near to zero political and socio-economic capital. In 2009, Myanmar's Consul-General in Hong Kong described the Rohingya boat people as 'ugly as ogres'.[15] This shows how many ordinary Rakhine Muslims have been denied a sense of humanity in the eyes of another group of human beings who have been their neighbours for generations.

---

14   USCIRF, 'Annual Report of the U.S. Commission on International Religious Freedom' (Washington, DC: USCIRF, 2011), pp. 36–37. Available at: http://www.uscirf.gov/sites/default/files/resources/book%20with%20cover%20 for%20web.pdf (accessed on 31 January 2018).

15   AFP, 'Myanmar envoy brands boatpeople "ugly as ogres"' (Agence France Press, 10 February 2009). Available from the Internet Archive: https:// web.archive.org/web/20140219173010/https://www.google.com/hostednews/ afp/article/ALeqM5j_x2afxfntqJUV3PuaTz6Jy12_Yg (accessed on 31 January 2018).

4 Myanmar's Scorched-Earth Campaign against the Rohingya

The precursors to the current violent uprooting of over 688,000 Rohingya people from Rakhine were the conflicts that started in northern Rakhine between Buddhists and Rohingya Muslims in June 2012. The trigger was an alleged gang rape and murder of a Rakhine Buddhist woman by Rohingya Muslims and the consequent killing of ten Muslims by Rakhine Buddhists in retaliation. Muslims in Maungdaw township, northern Rakhine, burnt some Buddhist houses on 8 June 2012. This unleashed a chain of events causing the deaths and burning of houses on both sides; tens of thousands of people, mostly Rohingya, were displaced and a state of emergency was declared. Many Rohingya were temporarily removed by security forces into makeshift refugee camps; cut off from the rest of the world, they have been languishing in those internment camps ever since. To add insult to the Rohingya injury, in July 2012 Myanmar President Thein Sein made a proposal to the UNHCR to resettle the Rohingya community in other countries; this was beyond belief and rejected[1] by the UN.

---

1   Saw Yan Naing, 'UNHCR Rejects Rohingya Resettlement Suggestion' (*The Irrawaddy*, 13 July 2012). Available at: https://www.irrawaddy.com/news/burma/unhcr-rejects-rohingya-resettlement-suggestion.html (accessed on 31 January 2018).

Racist vitriol against the Rohingya in the mainstream and on social media in Myanmar continued unabated. Buddhist majority Myanmar was going through a wave of anti-Muslim rage, thanks to some Buddhist hate preachers. One was the 45-year-old monk, Ashin Wirathu,[2] who gained widespread notoriety with his nationalist 'buy Buddhist and shop Buddhist' slogan. His 969 Movement (symbolising the virtues of the Buddha, Buddhist practices and the Buddhist community) encouraged Buddhists to excommunicate the Rohingya socio-economically; he also led a rally of monks in Mandalay in September 2012 to defend President Thein Sein's resettlement plan for the Rohingya.

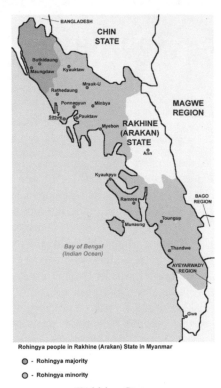

Rohingya people in Rakhine (Arakan) State in Myanmar

◎ - Rohingya majority

◯ - Rohingya minority

Rakhine State

---

2   Kate Hodal, 'Buddhist monk uses racism and rumours to spread hatred in Burma' (*The Guardian*, 18 April 2013). Available at: https://www.theguardian.com/world/2013/apr/18/buddhist-monk-spreads-hatred-burma (accessed on 31 January 2018).

In the aftermath of Suu Kyi's release in 2010, the military played a cat and mouse game with democracy. The Rohingya were not included in the 2014 census and most were not allowed to vote in the 2015 elections that brought the National League for Democracy (NLD) to power. Suu Kyi's party won and her NLD formed a government in March 2016. But in 'disciplined democracy'[3] the military-drafted constitution guaranteed that unelected military representatives took up 25 per cent of the seats in the Parliament (Hluttaw) and had a veto over constitutional change. Although banned from the presidency by the Myanmar constitution, the election made Suu Kyi *de facto* civilian head of Myanmar, holding offices of the state counsellor and minister for foreign affairs. To many it was just an extension of military rule under the garb of democracy, but the outside world appeared to be willing to live with this.

The role of Suu Kyi is ironic in the whole Rohingya saga. As a champion of democracy who suffered under military rule in the past, the international community expected she would bring, or at least make a serious effort to bring, a fresh air of ethical politics to Myanmar. However, she remained elusive on the continued suffering and violations of human rights endured by the Rohingya minority and made no attempt whatsoever to redress their plight. After the UN High Commission for Human Rights published a report mentioning that the Rohingya had been deprived of nationality and undergone systemic discrimination and severe restrictions on movement,[4] Suu Kyi told the special rapporteur that her government would avoid even using the term 'Rohingya'.[5]

In September 2016, her Office as the State Counsellor and the Kofi Annan Foundation established an Advisory Commission on Rakhine State[6] 'to examine the complex challenges facing Rakhine

---

3   BBC News, 'Myanmar's 2015 landmark elections explained' (BBC News, 3 December 2015). Available at: http://www.bbc.co.uk/news/world-asia-33547036 (accessed on 5 February 2018).

4   United Nations High Commissioner for Human Rights, 'Situation of human rights of Rohingya Muslims and other minorities in Myanmar' (New York: UN General Assembly, 20 June 2016). Available at: https://reliefweb.int/sites/reliefweb.int/files/resources/G1613541.pdf (accessed on 31 January 2018).

5   Reuters, 'Aung San Suu Kyi tells UN that the term "Rohingya" will be avoided' (*The Guardian*, 21 June 2016). Available at: https://www.theguardian.com/world/2016/jun/21/aung-san-suu-kyi-tells-un-that-the-term-rohingya-will-be-avoided (accessed on 31 January 2018).

6   Advisory Commission on Rakhine State, *Towards a Peaceful, Fair and Prosperous Future for the People of Rakhine*.

State and to propose responses to those challenges'. This raised the hopes of some as the majority of its members were from Myanmar. The Commission started working to find reasons and a way out of the crisis. However, the situation took a sharp turn for the worse when in October 2016 nine police officers were killed by armed men, believed by Myanmar officials to be from the ARSA. As many as 80,000 Rohingyas[7] were displaced in retaliation and many tried to enter Bangladesh after military operations that left scores of people dead. Myanmar was accused of seeking to 'ethnically cleanse the country of its Muslim minority' by a senior UN official. According to satellite images recorded on 10–18 November 2016, more than 1,200 homes were razed in villages inhabited by Rakhine's Muslim Rohingya minority.[8]

In March 2017, the Commission released a set of interim recommendations, raising yet more hope. The Advisory Commission submitted its final report to Myanmar's national authorities on 23 August with recommendations for 'urgent and sustained action on a number of fronts to prevent violence, maintain peace, foster reconciliation and offer a sense of hope to the State's hard-pressed population'.[9] But several hours after the publication of the Annan report on 25 August 2017, the ARSA attacked[10] twenty-four border guard posts, police stations and army bases in Maungdaw and some other townships in northern Rakhine that killed at least ten police officers and one soldier. For the Myanmar authorities this was a godsend as it destroyed any possibility of having to implement the Advisory Commission's recommendations. It is difficult to know what exactly triggered the ARSA to perform this callous act, or

---

7   Oliver Holmes, 'Myanmar seeking ethnic cleansing, says UN official as Rohingya flee persecution' (*The Guardian*, 24 November 2016). Available at: https://www.theguardian.com/world/2016/nov/24/rohingya-flee-to-bangladesh-to-escape-myanmar-military-strikes (accessed on 31 January 2018).

8   BBC News, 'Rohingya villages "destroyed" in Myanmar, images show' (BBC News, 21 November 2016). Available at: http://www.bbc.co.uk/news/world-asia-38049106 (accessed on 31 January 2018).

9   News Release, 'Advisory Commission on Rakhine State: Final Report' (Kofi Annan Foundation, 24 August 2017). Available at: http://www.kofiannanfoundation.org/mediation-and-crisis-resolution/rakhine-final-report/ (accessed on 31 January 2018).

10   Moe Myint, 'Muslim Militants Stage Major Attack in Rakhine' (*The Irrawaddy*, 25 August 2017). Available at: https://www.irrawaddy.com/news/burma/muslim-militants-stage-major-attack-rakhine.html (accessed on 31 January 2018).

whether there was anything more sinister behind this than to outdo Suu Kyi and Kofi Annan.

The inflamed situation led to a pre-planned counter operation with an unprecedented scorched-earth military campaign by Myanmar authorities against the Rohingya in northern Rakhine.[11] According to Amnesty International's report in mid-September 2017, soldiers, police and vigilante groups 'sometimes encircle a village and fire into the air before entering, but often just storm in and start firing in all directions, with people fleeing in panic'. Its analysis of active fire-detection data, satellite imagery, photographs and videos from the ground, as well as interviews with dozens of eyewitnesses in Myanmar and across the border in Bangladesh, 'shows how an orchestrated campaign of systematic burnings has targeted Rohingya villages across northern Rakhine State'. In legal terms, 'these are crimes against humanity', concluded Amnesty International.

Myanmar has denied UN accusations of ethnic cleansing. The government, the military and some Buddhist nationalists are trying to convince the world that their heartless and horrendous actions are just a clearance operation against the ARSA in Rakhine State and is necessary for national security. But, given their systematic persecution of this community since the military takeover in 1962, which has been on record, this simply does not wash. Compared to Myanmar's other highly equipped ethnic resistance groups in areas such as Kachin and Shan, the ARSA has proved itself to be a fringe group of disgruntled and ill-equipped individuals. Whatever the motive or timing of the ARSA attacks on that fateful night in late August 2017, the reality is Myanmar is using this as a pretext to exterminate the ethnic Rohingya Muslims from Rakhine.

The Rohingya have not only been denied citizenship and made stateless, they are even denied of their own ethnic identity; the Myanmar government and Suu Kyi's office are fearful of calling them Rohingya. But history has proved the Rohingya's legitimate right as children of the soil. The irony is most of them have been made 'refugees' in foreign countries, 'floating people' on the boats and so forth; the minority are 'encamped' in their own land! As Phil

---

11   'Myanmar: Scorched-earth campaign fuels ethnic cleansing of Rohingya from Rakhine State' (Amnesty International, 14 September 2017). Available at: https://www.amnesty.org/en/latest/news/2017/09/myanmar-scorched-earth-campaign-fuels-ethnic-cleansing-of-rohingya-from-rakhine-state/ (accessed on 31 January 2018).

Robertson, deputy director for Human Rights Watch in Asia, said: 'The Rohingya have little left besides their group name after years of statelessness, discriminatory restrictions on movement and access to life-sustaining services, and being targeted by a military subjecting them to ethnic cleansing and atrocities.'[12]

Yet their proud past in Arakan for a few centuries before the Burmese, and later British, takeover is a historical reality. They grew and flourished as a community along with other people from many backgrounds – Bengalis, Indians, Burmese and others – throughout their history. Their identity cannot simply be wiped out just because the Myanmar government, military and some chauvinist Buddhist monks want this. During European colonialism people migrated, were forcibly transported to, and settled in, various parts of the colonised world. Some became the majority, such as White Europeans in North America and the Australian continent. Others settled as minorities, such as Indians in South Africa. There can be community tensions, and this is not unnatural in any country, but no community should ever be denied its ethnic identity. Attempting to take away a people's identity is immoral and against international law. The fact that this is happening in twenty-first century Myanmar, a Buddhist majority country, under the eyes of the UN and the international community is astounding. It is an irony that the great Buddha himself was an Indian and many Buddhists migrated from Buddhist heartlands in India to East Asia and other places!

The Rohingya ethnic identity issue came to a flashpoint when Pope Francis visited Myanmar towards the end of November 2017. He was advised by Myanmar's Cardinal Bo against using the word 'Rohingya' or the 'R word'[13] when he would visit the country. Pope Francis has proved himself to be a renowned defender of human rights and has spoken of 'the persecution of our Rohingya brothers and sisters'. But although he spoke for 'peace based on respect for the dignity and rights of each member of society', he capitulated

---

12   Philip Pullella, 'Pope advised not to use term "Rohingya" in Myanmar but rights groups disagree' (Reuters, 15 November 2017). Available at: https://uk.reuters.com/article/uk-pope-myanmar-rohingya/pope-advised-not-to-use-term-rohingya-in-myanmar-but-rights-groups-disagree-idUKKBN1DF20C (accessed on 31 January 2018).

13   Christopher Lamb, 'Pope Must Avoid Mentioning "Rohingya" on Visit to Buddhist-Majority Myanmar' (The Tablet, 17 November 2017). Available at: http://www.thetablet.co.uk/news/8100/0/pope-must-avoid-mentioning-rohingya-on-visit-to-buddhist-majority-myanmar- (accessed on 31 January 2018).

in Naypyidaw and 'did not use the word "Rohingya" or mention allegations that the Burmese military is engaged in a campaign of ethnic cleansing and genocide against them'.[14] Maybe it was the Naypyidaw effect, but he missed an opportunity of speaking truth to power, although he attempted to recover lost ground during the next leg of his visit in Bangladesh. Disappointment from the Rohingya and human rights groups aside, this will be seen as dilution of his moral authority by many.

Aung San Suu Kyi is a politician in an age when some very senior politicians across the world do not care about public ethics. The difference is, during her sufferings at the hands of the Burmese military, she championed democracy and human rights and as a result received global recognition including the Nobel Peace Prize and other prestigious awards. On the Rohingya issue, the civilised world expected a higher level of moral courage and statesmanship from her. The military has its agenda of controlling the country and there is mistrust in her political marriage between NLD and the military; Aung San Suu Kyi still does not have enough room for manoeuvre in running the country. However, she has also done virtually nothing to challenge the dangerous myths surrounding the Rohingya or to build bridges between communities.

Her own office enthusiastically uses the term 'Bengali' for the Rohingya and she has done little to correct this. There is a myth that that the military would find any excuse to retake direct control of the country. This is understandable, but highly unlikely as the current 'political system in Burma now is entirely the creation of the military.'[15] Suu Kyi's position as State Counsellor provides cover for the Myanmar military and protects them from the domestic and internal pressure they had faced in the past. The military's total grip on the country has made democracy meaningless, as it has the power to do anything. This may also be used by some in the international community as an excuse for their own inaction in meaningfully helping the Rohingya.

---

14   Roland Oliphant, 'Pope avoids using term "Rohingya" in Burma address, as he urges respect "for each ethnicity and its identity"' (*The Telegraph*, 28 November 2017). Available at: http://www.telegraph.co.uk/news/2017/11/28/pope-avoids-using-term-rohingya-burma-address-urges-respect/ (accessed on 31 January 2018).

15   Burma Briefing, 'The military coup threat myth' (Burma Campaign UK, October 2017). Available at: http://burmacampaign.org.uk/media/The-military-coup-threat-myth.pdf (accessed on 5 February 2018).

Does Suu Kyi have a problem with Muslims? Well, her past remarks about 'global Muslim power'[16] and the reported exclusion of Muslims[17] by the NLD from its list of candidates for the November 2015 election suggest that she personally shares anti-Muslim prejudices. This came into public view when in March 2016, after the BBC *Today* presenter Mishal Husain gave Suu Kyi a rough ride during an interview, the latter was reported to have 'lost her composure and was heard to mutter off-air: "No one told me I was going to be interviewed by a Muslim"'.[18]

If a minority community in her own country is in effect annihilated and ethnically cleansed from the land then should she not find ways to put a brake on it? Politicians should sometimes take a moral stand, show leadership and seriously try to find innovative ways to avert gross injustices. Her words and actions so far prove she has not made any attempt whatsoever to reconcile military antagonism towards the Rohingya and their right to live in Myanmar with dignity. Her neo-populist[19] stance at the Asia Europe Foreign Ministers meeting at Naypyidaw on 20 November 2017, calling the ARSA 'extremist Bengali terrorists' and suggesting illegal migration from Bangladesh as an existential threat to Myanmar, was mind-boggling! Anyone who knows anything about the ARSA would be aware that this tiny self-serving fringe group does not represent the Rohingya people, let alone Bengalis.

The West invested heavily in Suu Kyi for a long time in its strategic relationship with Myanmar. But her failure to act on the Rohingya crisis has destroyed the 'saintly' myth around her.[20] Perhaps she was outmanoeuvred by the military, or maybe she was not worth

---

16   Haroon Siddique, 'Burma sectarian violence motivated by fear, says Aung San Suu Kyi' (*The Guardian*, 24 October 2013). Available at: https://www. theguardian.com/world/2013/oct/24/burma-sectarian-violence-fear-aung-san-suu-kyi (accessed on 31 January 2018).

17   Jonah Fisher, 'Aung San Suu Kyi's party excludes Muslim candidates' (BBC News, 8 September 2015). Available at: http://www.bbc.co.uk/news/world-asia-34182489 (accessed on 31 January 2018).

18   Nicola Harley, 'Aung San Suu Kyi in anti-Muslim spat with BBC presenter' (*The Telegraph*, 25 March 2016). Available at: http://www.telegraph. co.uk/news/2016/03/25/aung-san-suu-kyi-in-anti-muslim-spat-with-bbc-presenter/ (accessed on 31 January 2018).

19   David Scott Mathieson, 'Suu Kyi takes a populist, paranoid turn' (*Asia Times*, 21 November 2017). Available at: http://www.atimes.com/article/suu-kyi-takes-populist-paranoid-turn/ (accessed on 31 January 2018).

20   Alan Davis, 'The west wanted Aung San Suu Kyi to be a saint. It's no surprise she is not' (*The Guardian*, 19 September 2017). Available at: https://

the adulation she received, but apparently lacking moral fibre many people think her political career may now be on the wane as well. Suu Kyi has been hugely criticised internationally in recent times. The Irish musician and humanitarian activist Bob Geldof called her 'a hand maiden to genocide'[21] and returned his Freedom of the City of Dublin award in protest over her response to the repression of Rohingya Muslims. She was stripped of her Freedom of Oxford award,[22] the city's highest honour, because of her inaction in the face of oppression of the minority Rohingya population.

However, while Suu Kyi deserves huge criticism, the architect of the Rohingya destruction is the military. For more than fifty years the military, despite rough transitions of leadership, stayed united and kept absolute power by handling their opponents with an iron fist. The military has proved to be resilient and has outsmarted all opposition – internal and external. The main villain now is its current head, General Min Aung Hlaing.

In its new and tortuous journey towards democracy, the destruction of a community does not bode well for Myanmar. The civilian–military government may consider this a clever tactic in the short-term to bring harmony and prosperity to a majority Buddhist country, but this will definitely prove dangerous in the long run. Injustice can never bring good in human society and it may well destroy Myanmar's own credibility and ignite 'dangerous religious and ethnic fissures', affecting 'the security of the region'.[23]

By the beginning of December 2017, the number of Rohingya refugees who had fled to Bangladesh from Myanmar since 25 August had reached 688,000. A national English-language daily in Bangladesh, the *Dhaka Tribune*, reported on 18 January 2018 that 'a

---

www.theguardian.com/commentisfree/2017/sep/19/west-aung-san-suu-kyi-saint-nobel-rohingya (accessed on 31 January 2018).

21   Padraic Halpin, 'Bob Geldof calls Aung San Suu Kyi "handmaiden to genocide"' (Reuters, 13 November 2017). Available at: https://www.reuters.com/article/us-myanmar-rohingya-geldof/bob-geldof-calls-aung-san-suu-kyi-handmaiden-to-genocide-idUSKBN1DD0X6 (accessed on 31 January 2018).

22   Telegraph Reporters, 'Aung San Suu Kyi stripped of her Freedom of Oxford award' (*The Telegraph*, 27 November 2017). Available at: http://www.telegraph.co.uk/news/2017/11/27/aung-san-suu-kyi-stripped-freedom-oxford-award/ (accessed on 31 January 2018).

23   Sahar Khan, 'The Danger of Linking the Rohingya Crisis to Terrorism' (The Diplomat, 13 October 2017). Available at: https://thediplomat.com/2017/10/the-danger-of-linking-the-rohingya-crisis-to-terrorism/ (accessed on 31 January 2018).

total [of] 1,010,714 Rohingyas have registered their biometric data with the Bangladeshi government since September 12, 2017',[24] this is around two-thirds of their entire population![25] This is probably Myanmar's 'Final Solution' *vis-à-vis* the Rohingya in their midst, and the Muslim situation in southern Rakhine and other places is becoming more precarious with each passing day.

In mid-January 2018, news about Bangladesh and Myanmar agreeing a timeframe for repatriating the Rohingya from Bangladesh to Myanmar created concerns amongst aid agencies.[26] Myanmar's Foreign Secretary, U Myint Thu, told BBC Burmese: 'The repatriation process will commence on 23 January.' In response, the UN Secretary-General António Guterres told reporters: 'The worst would be to move these people from camps in Bangladesh to camps in Myanmar [Burma], keeping an artificial situation for a long time and not allowing for them to regain their normal lives'.[27]

The failure of the Myanmar government to take the repatriation of Rohingya refugees seriously was confirmed in March 2018 when from a list of over 8,000 people who were willing to return home, submitted by the Bangladeshi government, only 374 were approved. 'Myanmar blamed Bangladesh for the slow process, accusing its neighbour of submitting missing or "incomplete" information'. and even if the Rohingya returned home they would be housed in 'temporary housing camps' since many of Rohingya villages have been bulldozed, 'with large concrete structures and military bases being built in their place.' Clearly the worst fears of the UN and aid agencies have been realised.[28]

---

24   Tarek Mahmud, 'Over one million Rohingyas get biometric registration' (*Dhaka Tribune*, 18 January 2018). Available at: http://www.dhakatribune. com/bangladesh/2018/01/18/one-million-rohingyas-get-biometric-registration/ (accessed on 13 February 2018).

25   Justin Rowlatt, 'Could Aung San Suu Kyi face Rohingya genocide charges?' (BBC News, 18 December 2017). Available at: http://www.bbc.co.uk/ news/world-asia-42335018 (accessed on 31 January 2018).

26   BBC News, 'Rohingya crisis: Bangladesh and Myanmar agree repatriation timeframe' (BBC News, 16 January 2018). Available at: http://www.bbc.com/ news/world-asia-42699602 (accessed on 31 January 2018).

27   HRW, 'Burma/Bangladesh: Return Plan Endangers Refugees' (Human Rights Watch, 23 January 2018). Available at: https://www.hrw.org/news/ 2018/01/23/burma/bangladesh-return-plan-endangers-refugees (accessed on 31 January 2018).

28   Hannah Ellis-Petersen, 'Myanmar willing to take back fewer than 400 Rohingya refugees' (The Guardian, 15 March 2018). Available at: https://www. theguardian.com/world/2018/mar/15/myanmar-willing-to-take-back-fewer-than-400-rohingya-refugees-bangladesh (accessed on 18 March 2018).

5 A Human Tragedy with Debasement of Women and Children

The completely man-made human tragedy that has befallen the Rohingya in Myanmar is beyond belief. The horrors faced and recounted by adults, mainly women, and children who have managed to complete the arduous journey to Bangladesh will shock anyone who listens to them. A report published by Save the Children International, *Horrors I will never forget*,[1] written after its Chief Executive visited Rohingya refugee camps in Bangladesh's Cox's Bazar in October 2017, gives the 'testimonies of children who have seen and suffered senseless acts of violence in this crisis, along with testimonies from families and friends who recount the stories that others cannot tell for themselves due to trauma, separation or death.'

The mass exodus of Rohingya people to the sprawling camps of Cox's Bazar, Bangladesh after 25 August 2017 consists mostly of pregnant women, the elderly and children. So far 378,000 children have fled northern Rakhine where many have witnessed horrific violence no child should ever see.[2] No one knows how long the

---

1   Claire Mason and Mark Kaye, *Horrors I Will Never Forget* (London: Save the Children International, 2017). Available at: http://www.savethechildren. org.au/__data/assets/pdf_file/0005/242933/Horrors-I-Will-Never-Forget.pdf (accessed on 1 February 2018).

2   Ian Woolverton, 'In the name of humanity, don't look away from the plight of the Rohingya people' (*The Guardian*, 18 December 2017). Available at: https://

shanty structures covered with fragile plastic sheet or tin roofing will be the home of these terror-stricken people, but at least they are free from the threat of Myanmar soldiers, police and the Rakhine Buddhist mobs! Children wearing dirty clothes walk barefoot through dirty puddles, help their elders and even play in safety. With changing weather and the onset of the monsoon season there is huge concern for the wellbeing of malnourished children with weak immune systems. Unless living conditions are significantly improved, their health will worsen by the time the next monsoon pours water from Bangladesh's sky. It is a race against time for the Rohingya people's physical space, protection from weather, health and their children's education. International help is coming, but sadly at a slow pace.

Rape and sexual assault are often used as techniques to dehumanise the enemy in war, or by vile people when they are in control. There is now sufficient evidence to demonstrate that systematic mass rape[3] has been used as a weapon by the Burmese

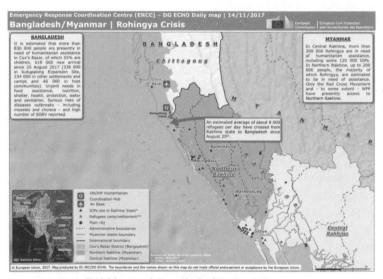

Rakhine and Bangladesh's Cox's Bazar

www.theguardian.com/commentisfree/2017/dec/18/in-the-name-of-humanity-dont-look-away-from-the-plight-of-the-rohingya-people (accessed on 1 February 2018).

3   Patrick Wintour, 'UK drags heels on sending mass rape investigators to Myanmar' (*The Guardian*, 5 November 2017). Available at: https://www.theguardian.com/world/2017/nov/05/uk-yet-to-send-team-to-myanmar-to-gather-evidence (accessed on 1 February 2018).

military against the Rohingya minority. 'The (Myanmar) military has clearly used rape as one of a range of horrific methods of ethnic cleansing against the Rohingya',[4] said a sexual violence expert with Human Rights Watch (HRW). Myanmar dismisses such accusations, saying it was just fighting insurgents. But experts are aware that the ARSA is ill-prepared to wage an insurgency and has no root in the Rohingya community. The Myanmar establishment is just making a flimsy excuse to viciously drive the Rohingya out of their homeland and cause them maximum humiliation. Human Rights Watch cited first-hand interviews with fifty-two Rohingya women and girls who fled to Bangladesh.[5] These barbaric acts of violence have left countless women and girls physically brutalised and traumatised, and many women and girls do not seek medical care for sexual violence due to shame and fear.

Children were not spared from sexual violence either; even a 9-year-old girl[6] who received medical treatment by Médecins Sans Frontières at its Kutupalong health facility's sexual and reproductive health unit in Cox's Bazar was raped. These accounts confirm the stories of numerous refugees who describe similar incidents of mass rape, with many saying some victims were subsequently killed. Myanmar's army usually denies all allegations of rape and killings by security forces.

Film star Angelina Jolie, a special envoy of the United Nations High Commissioner for Refugees (UNHCR), condemned[7] the sexual violence inflicted on Rohingya women. The UN special envoy on sexual violence in conflict, Pramila Patten, said sexual violence

---

4   News Desk, 'Myanmar using rape as weapon against Rohingya' (The New Paper, 21 October 2017). Available at: http://www.tnp.sg/news/world/myanmar-using-rape-weapon-against-rohingya (accessed on 1 February 2018).

5   Esha Sarai 'HRW Report: Rohingya Women Gang Raped by Myanmar Soldiers' (Voice of America, 16 November 2017). Available at: https://www.voanews.com/a/hrw-rohingya-women-gang--raped-by-soldiers/4117729.html (accessed on 1 February 2018).

6   Fiona MacGregor, 'Rohingya girls under 10 raped while fleeing Myanmar, charity says' (The Guardian, 25 October 2017). Available at: https://www.theguardian.com/world/2017/oct/25/rohingya-children-fled-myanmar-violence-charity (accessed on 1 February 2018).

7   Ruma Paul, 'Angelina Jolie condemns sexual violence against Rohingya women refugees' (Reuters, 16 November 2017). Available at: https://www.reuters.com/article/us-myanmar-rohingya/angelina-jolie-condemns-sexual-violence-against-rohingya-women-refugees-idUSKBN1DG0V9 (accessed on 1 February 2018).

was 'being commanded, orchestrated and perpetrated by the Armed Forces of Myanmar.' In a meeting with NATO Secretary-General Jens Stoltenberg in January 2018,[8] Jolie specifically addressed the plight of the Rohingya and the response of many governments around the world: 'I'm very concerned about the Rohingya, I'm very angry at the response ... I'm very concerned about the stories of the 10-year old girls being raped,' she said. 'We should all hang our head on how little we have been able to do'. A British Foreign Office team, set up in 2012 by then foreign secretary William Hague and Angelina Jolie to highlight the pervasive use of sexual violence in conflict[9] needs to be effective in reporting from Myanmar's refugee camps. The Foreign Office needs to activate its team fully so it can collect testimonies from survivors and victims in order to assemble the cases of mass rape and eventually bring the perpetrators to the International Criminal Court.

In late November 2017, the UN Committee on the Elimination of Discrimination against Women (CEDAW) called on Myanmar[10] to provide information on a range of issues surrounding alleged instances of violence against women and girls in northern Rakhine State in recent months. The request included information concerning cases of sexual violence, including rape, against Rohingya women and girls by the state security forces.

What makes the crisis even more heartrending is that almost 60 per cent of those fleeing Myanmar are children.[11] One in five Rohingya children under the age of five[12] is estimated to be acutely

8   Reuters Staff, 'Angelina Jolie urges NATO to tackle sexual violence in war' (Reuters, 31 January 2018). Available at: https://www.reuters.com/article/us-nato-violence-jolie/angelina-jolie-urges-nato-to-tackle-sexual-violence-in-war-idUSKBN1FK26Q (accessed on 1 February 2018).

9   Wintour, 'UK drags heels on sending mass rape investigators to Myanmar'.

10   Press Release, 'Myanmar: UN experts request exceptional report on situation of women and girls from northern Rakhine State' (Office of the United Nations High Commissioner for Human Rights, 28 November 2017). Available at: http://www.ohchr.org/EN/NewsEvents/Pages/DisplayNews.aspx?NewsID=22459&LangID=E (accessed on 1 February 2018).

11   Theirworld, 'Rohingya refugee children need urgent help to deal with their trauma' (ReliefWeb, 26 September 2017). Available at: https://reliefweb.int/report/bangladesh/rohingya-refugee-children-need-urgent-help-deal-their-trauma (accessed on 1 February 2018).

12   Stephanie Nebehay, 'Rohingya refugee children in Bangladesh in dire state: UNICEF' (Reuters, 20 October 2017). Available at: https://www.reuters.com/article/us-myanmar-rohingya-children/rohingya-refugee-children-in-bangladesh-in-dire-state-unicef-idUSKBN1CP00B (accessed on 1 February 2018).

malnourished, requiring medical attention. Nearly 340,000 in these camps are 'outcast and desperate'[13] in squalid conditions without adequate access to food, water and healthcare. What can be more brutal in human society than treating children so cruelly? The Rohingya crisis has been labelled as a 'children's crisis'.[14] The head of the world's largest humanitarian network, Elhadj As Sy, said, 'Never have I seen so many children in a crisis [...] Children who have seen things that a child should never witness.'[15]

Most of the children have been exposed to extreme trauma, as they have witnessed their dearest ones killed or tortured and their homes burned. Some spent many days walking through the rainforest to reach safety. Médecins Sans Frontières says dozens of Rohingya girls have been given medical and psychological support[16] at one of its sexual and reproductive health units. Many children at the camps are still separated from their families and the numbers are still growing. The stronger ones help themselves and their families survive by carrying relief and water on their shoulders. Some are orphans, while others became lost during the journey from Myanmar. With so many undocumented children living without their parents, aid workers are worried about cases of abuse and trafficking. Children affected by war or violence go through inexplicable stress and anguish. When they are exposed to periods of prolonged hunger, poverty and fear, as well as chronic neglect and abuse, their stress levels rise significantly. This may give rise to disturbing consequences, with disorders in their physical and mental health later on in life.

UNHCR and other humanitarian groups that are working with children should involve professional and empathic volunteers with teaching (or at least social work) backgrounds to work with children for their overall wellbeing. Safeguarding children from mindless criminals who may try to cash in from trafficking, sexual abuse,

---

13   Lydia Smith, 'Rohingya crisis: Nearly 340,000 children 'outcast and desperate' in squalid Bangladesh camps, Unicef warns' (*The Independent*, 22 October 2017). Available at: http://www.independent.co.uk/news/world/asia/ rohingya-crisis-children-outcast-desperate-squalid-conditions-bangladesh-camps-unicef-a8013501.html (accessed on 1 February 2018).

14   Poppy McPherson, '"I miss them so much": Myanmar's lost Rohingya children plead for their parents' (*The Guardian*, 5 November 2017). Available at: https://www.theguardian.com/world/2017/nov/05/i-miss-them-so-much-myanmars-lost-rohingya-children-plead-for-their-parents (accessed on 1 February 2018).

15   McPherson, 'World failing Myanmar's Rohingya Muslims'.

16   MacGregor, 'Rohingya girls under 10 raped while fleeing Myanmar'.

pornography, child labour and child marriage should, of course, be the number one priority. However, children should be given the basic opportunity to express themselves and their traumatic experiences orally and creatively in a safe environment. This may give a glimpse as to what is going on in their minds and will allow compassionate adults to give them realistic optimism to rebuild their lives.

Children are born innocent and are inherently vulnerable; they deserve physical protection, safety, love and psychological care as well as comfort and counselling in the adult world. They must be housed close to people they are comfortable with and they have the basic right to be given age-appropriate education, training and life skills so that they can survive in previously unknown environments and prepare for a dignified life.

Expressing huge concern for the plight of Rohingya children fleeing Myanmar, the Nobel Laureate Kailash Satyarthi, India's foremost children's rights activist, urged: 'If any child is being victimised during the current Rohingya crisis in Myanmar, then this is the moral responsibility of the world community to resolve this crisis.'[17]

---

17   FP Staff, 'Kailash Satyarthi expresses concern over Rohingya children's plight, seeks UN intervention' (FirstPost, 3 October 2017). Available at: http://www.firstpost.com/india/kailash-satyarthi-expresses-concern-over-rohingya-childrens-plight-seeks-un-intervention-4106993.html (accessed on 1 February 2018).

6 Genocide by All Counts

Decades of virulent propaganda designed to poison ordinary Buddhist minds against the Rohingya, state-sponsored persecution, denial of their identity as well as systemic misinformation and starving Rohingya of basic needs and opportunities in life by the Myanmar regime have turned them into a pariah people and made normal life impossible. Myanmar's treatment of the Rohingya fits in with most of the eight stages of Genocide as defined by Professor Gregory Stanton of Genocide Watch.[1] According to him, these are: classification, symbolisation, dehumanisation, organisation, polarisation preparation, extermination and denial of a people.

Nobel Laureate Amartya Sen described the treatment of the Rohingya as a 'slow genocide'[2] as early as in November 2014. 'It is not only about an evil government doing very nasty things' he said, but an 'evil government first changing the character of the people'. In 2015, in a legal document on the human rights situation in Myanmar's Rakhine State, the Allard K. Lowenstein International Human Rights Clinic at Yale Law School found strong evidence of genocide[3] against

---

1   Gregory H. Stanton, 'The 8 Stages of Genocide' (Genocide Watch, 1998). Available at: http://www.genocidewatch.org/aboutgenocide/8stagesofgenocide. html (accessed on 1 February 2018).

2   Maung Zarni, 'The Slow Genocide of the Rohingya by Amartya Sen' (Harvard University, November 2014. Posted 21 May 2016). Available at: https://www.youtube.com/watch?v=ugHhAwARb98&feature=youtu.be (accessed on 1 February 2018).

3   Yale Law School, 'Clinic Study Finds Evidence of Genocide in Myanmar' (Yale Law School, 29 October 2015). Available at: https://law.yale.edu/yls-today/

the Rohingya population. It recommended that the UN Human Rights Council establish a Commission of Inquiry to 'conduct an urgent, comprehensive, and independent investigation of the human rights situation in Rakhine State.'

After a 12-month research study, the International State Crime Initiative (ISCI) of the Queen Mary University of London published a report, *Countdown to Annihilation: Genocide in Myanmar*, concluding that 'genocide is taking place in Myanmar' and warned of 'the serious and present danger of the annihilation of the country's Rohingya population.'[4] The report found 'compelling evidence of State-led policies, laws and strategies of genocidal persecution stretching back over 30 years, and of the Myanmar State coordinating with Rakhine ultra-nationalists, racist monks and its own security forces in a genocidal process against the Rohingya.'[5]

Professor Green and her team used Daniel Feierstein's six-stage categorisation of genocide:[6] stigmatisation and dehumanisation; harassment, violence and terror; isolation and segregation; systematic weakening of the target group; mass annihilation; erasure of the target group from collective history. The ISCI documented in detail the evidence for genocide, its historical genesis and the political, social and economic conditions in which it emerged. It identified the architects of the genocide as Myanmar state officials and security forces, Rakhine nationalist leaders and Buddhist monks; it pointed to a significant degree of coordination between these agencies in the pursuit of eliminating the Rohingya from Myanmar's political landscape. In conclusion, the report warned that 'decades of persecution have taken on a new and intensified form since the mass killings in 2012'[7] and concluded that the Rohingya had been suffering the first four of the six stages of genocide as a prelude to the last two – mass annihilation and

---

news/clinic-study-finds-evidence-genocide-myanmar (accessed on 1 February 2018).

4   Penny Green, Thomas MacManus and Alicia de la Cour Venning, *Countdown to Annihilation: Genocide in Myanmar* (London: International State Crime Initiative, 2015), p. 16. Available at: http://statecrime.org/data/2015/10/ISCI-Rohingya-Report-PUBLISHED-VERSION.pdf (accessed on 1 February 2018).

5   Ibid. p. 15.

6   Daniel Feierstein, *Genocide as Social Practice: Reorganising Society under the Nazis and Argentina's Military Juntas* (New Brunswick, NJ: Rutgers University Press, 2014), pp. 110–21.

7   Green, MacManus and de la Cour Venning, *Countdown to Annihilation*, p. 99.

erasure. Very few have any doubt that what has happened since August 2017 has all but completed the last two stages of genocide.

After a two year investigation into the root causes of these appalling events, Amnesty International produced a report, *'Caged Without a Roof': Apartheid in Myanmar's Rakhine State*,[8] in November 2017. It revealed how Myanmar's authorities 'have confined the Rohingya to what is effectively an open-air prison through a vicious system of institutionalised discrimination and segregation that severely restricts their human rights. It's a system that affects their freedom of movement, their ability to access adequate food and healthcare, and their right to an education.'[9] The human rights body concluded that this treatment amounts to apartheid, defined by The Rome Statute of the International Criminal Court as a crime against humanity.[10]

In a debate about the Rohingya people in the British parliament in November 2017, British Foreign Secretary Boris Johnson told the House of Commons that the British government had 'recently received evidence of a very troubling kind, and [we will] make sure that such testimony [...] is collated and used so that the proper judicial authorities can determine whether indeed it answers to the definition of genocide.'[11] It is imperative this is pursued robustly without any failing. A BBC *Newsnight* documentary,[12] 'Rohingya crisis: The Tula

---

8   Amnesty International *'Caged Without a Roof': Apartheid in Myanmar's Rakhine State* (London: Amnesty International, 2017). Available at: https://www.amnesty.org/download/Documents/ASA1674842017ENGLISH.PDF   (accessed on 1 February 2018).

9   Press Release, '"Caged Without a Roof": Apartheid in Myanmar's Rakhine State' (Amnesty International, 2017). Available at: https://www.amnesty.org/en/latest/news/2017/11/myanmar-apartheid-in-rakhine-state/ (accessed on 1 February 2018).

10   Apartheid is conduct imposing and maintaining a regime of systematic oppression and domination by one racial group over another within a country. It's a system that's upheld by legislative and administrative measures, policies and practices all designed to isolate a racial group – in this case the Rohingya – to deny their human rights and to stop them from participating in the political, social and economic life of a country.

11   Adam Lusher, 'Burma-Rohingya Crisis: UK has received "very troubling" evidence that might suggest "genocide" has been committed' (*The Independent*, 21 November 2017). Available at: http://www.independent.co.uk/news/world/asia/burma-rohingya-crisis-uk-evidence-genocide-boris-johnson-muslims-aung-san-suu-kyi-amnesty-a8067911.html (accessed on 1 February 2018).

12   BBC *Newsnight*, 'Rohingya crisis: The Tula Toli massacre' (BBC, 14 November 2017). Available at: https://www.youtube.com/watch?v=HRp0o0fzB2I (accessed on 1 February 2018).

Toli massacre', broadcast on 14 November 2017 revealed how the Myanmar army had committed a 'monstrous crime' by killing the villagers of Tula Toli, raping women and burning people and were preparing for violence even before the ARSA attacks on 25 August.

The UN designation of Myanmar's treatment of the Rohingya as 'ethnic cleansing' has been widely echoed around the world by prominent individuals and organisations. Others have termed it a monstrous crime, apartheid, annihilation, a crime against humanity, the destruction of Rohingya people and genocide. There is now mounting evidence that the Rohingya have been enduring systemic discrimination, denial of rights such as education and health, organised violence and the organised killing, rape and burning of people as well as the torching of houses to drive them out of their homes.

Myanmar continues to refuse the UN-mandated fact-finding mission in Rakhine State. The State Counsellor preferred to invite Kofi Annan to lead the Advisory Commission, claiming that international or UN involvement would contribute to fuelling further tensions in Rakhine. The Advisory Commission produced some useful observations and recommendations, although it did not address many of the core issues that the Rohingya have been struggling with. But it was all thrown out of the window on 25 August 2017 in the aftermath of the ARSA attacks and subsequent inhuman Myanmar onslaught on the Rohingya. The UN should now step in forcefully and start formally assessing whether what the Rohingyas have been subjected to so far constitutes 'crimes against humanity' or 'genocide'. Both are serious; the former is a 'deliberate act, typically as part of a systematic campaign, that causes human suffering or death on a large scale'; the latter the 'deliberate killing of a large group of people, especially those of a particular nation or ethnic group'.

In early November, Human Rights Watch urged the UN Security Council to refer Burma to the International Criminal Court (ICC) and UN member countries to pursue processes for gathering criminal evidence to advance prosecutions.[13] The UN High Commissioner for Human Rights, Zeid Ra'ad al-Hussein, suggested on 5 December 2017 that genocide against Rohingya Muslims by Myanmar cannot be ruled out.[14] He urged the Council to request that the UN

---

13   HRW, 'UN Security Council: Refer Burma to the ICC' (Human Rights Watch, 3 November 2017). Available at: https://www.hrw.org/news/2017/11/03/un-security-council-refer-burma-icc (accessed on 5 February 2018).

14   BBC News, 'Rohingya crisis: UN rights chief "cannot rule out genocide"'.

General Assembly set up a mechanism 'to assist individual criminal investigations of those responsible'. An unequivocal use of the term 'genocide' to describe the orchestrated state killings of the Rohingya would significantly increase international pressure on Myanmar. In an interview for BBC *Panorama* broadcast on 18 December 2017, al-Hussein reiterated that 'he doesn't rule out the possibility that civilian leader Aung San Suu Kyi and the head of the armed forces Gen Aung Min Hlaing, could find themselves in the dock on genocide charges sometime in the future'.[15]

A few isolated terrorist attacks by the ARSA were used as an excuse to commit crimes against humanity and unleash a campaign of ethnic cleansing and genocide on the entire Rohingya population. Satellite images have confirmed that many areas of Rakhine were burned to ashes and countless Rohingya have lost everything they had. The refugees' horrible tales of torture and persecution, of family members being killed before their very eyes and babies thrown into fires in front of mothers, of mass rapes of Rohingya women and girls both by the Myanmar army and the violent Rakhine Buddhist mobs have echoed around the vast camps of Cox's Bazar. The documentation process by various international agencies has only just begun, but hopefully in 2018 many of them will be published.

The world community is gradually coming to terms with the reality that the systemic mistreatment of the Rohingya that began in the 1960s has given rise to the indiscriminate killing, the debasement of women and children, the burning of homes and the uprooting of most of the population from their homeland that took place in the first few weeks after 25 August 2017. The fact that this is happening in the twenty-first century shames us all. As acts of genocide can only be ascertained by a court, the head of the UN's watchdog for human rights has called for an international criminal investigation into the perpetrators of what he has called the 'shockingly brutal attacks' against the Rohingya ethnic group in Myanmar. Given all the available evidence, the UN should now call a spade a spade, designate the Rohingya persecution as genocide and act to protect the minority community in the name of humanity. The UN needs to immediately and urgently activate its procedures regarding the committing of genocide and hold the Myanmar government and the army to account.

---

15   BBC *Panorama*, 'Myanmar: The Hidden Truth' (BBC, 23 December 2017). Available at: http://www.bbc.co.uk/programmes/b09kdnwb (accessed on 1 February 2018). This programme is available to view in the UK only.

The common saying, 'justice delayed is justice denied' is apt in the case of the Rohingya. However, even in our imperfect world, although justice may not be seen in one's lifetime it often arrives in the end and in various forms. Ratko Mladić, the Bosnian Serb former general and the 'butcher of Bosnia', and his colleagues were caught after many tearful years from Bosnian mothers and persistent attempts by many morally upright people to apprehend him. The EU was convinced that what had been inflicted on the Bosnian Muslims was genocide and the perpetrators of the crimes against Bosniaks were caught and punished. Mladić himself was caught in 2011 and in November 2017 he was committed to life imprisonment for his crimes. After over two decades, justice was finally served!

7 Geo-Political Competition

Myanmar is strategically located on the eastern rim of the Indian Ocean. As the centre of gravity of the world is gradually moving to the East, global interest in Myanmar has significantly increased in recent years, especially after the start of its so-called democratisation process. The military had a monopoly over everything in Myanmar, and has been fighting insurgency groups in the south, east and north with brutal force. Following the military orchestrated transition after the 2015 elections, democracy in Myanmar has become a red herring. The military is bluffing the international community, while global and regional powers appear impatient in courting favour with its rulers.

The United States of America

After the demise of communism in 1989, America emerged as the undisputed global super power with unmatched hard power as well as soft power. But in 2001, the unexpected terrorist attacks on 9/11 changed everything. In the aftermath of the atrocity there was global sympathy for the US, though many around the world soon developed a dislike for America after President Bush illegally invaded and occupied an Arab country, Iraq, in 2003. The financial crisis of 2007–8 that began with a crisis in the sub-prime mortgage market in the US shattered the invincibility of its economy and 'the global financial crisis […] turned the spotlight to America's declining economic prowess. Once the fearsome colossus, many now see the financially-strapped U.S. as a great power in decline.'[1] However, America's political, economic, and military power is still unmatched in the world and will continue to be for some time to come.

America has always been a Eurocentric country, but following the Indian Ocean earthquake and tsunami in December 2004 it started to concentrate more on the Indian Ocean and western Pacific region. President Obama's arrival into office in January 2009 and his declaration of America's strategic pivot in Asia two years later was apparently designed 'to restore and then enhance its traditional level of engagement' in the region.[2] Writing about Myanmar in his book *Monsoon*, published in 2011, Robert D. Kaplan observed that: 'Democracy will not solve Burma's dilemma of being a mini-empire of nationalities, even if it does open the door to a compromise. More than that, however, Burma's hill tribes are part of a new and larger canvas of geo-politics'.[3] As Burma was opening to democracy, Obama understood the importance of Myanmar's strategic location and visited the country in 2012. All this alerted China and India of American intentions in Asia, and both countries are covetous of its abundant reserves of oil, zinc, copper, precious stones, timber, and hydropower. So, while Myanmar is vital for America's interest in Asia, it is also essential to both China and India as neighbours. Herein lies the geo-political tussle.

America's humanitarian assistance helped post-war Europe and Japan to stand on their own feet economically. Also, through its aid budget it has helped many countries in the world. But where its political and strategic interests take preference, it has ruthlessly exploited such situations. For example, when Afghanistan was invaded and occupied by the Soviet Union in the late 1970s, America's primary interest was to defeat communism – not to help the Afghans or to build a better Afghanistan. The focus of America and its allies to drive the Soviets from the rugged mountains of Afghanistan in 1980s and 1990s without looking to the future development of the region sowed the seeds of modern nihilistic terrorism and has been haunting the Muslim world ever since.

---

1   Richard Wike, 'From Hyperpower to Declining Power' (Pew Research Center, 7 September 2011). Available at: http://www.pewglobal.org/2011/09/07/from-hyperpower-to-declining-power/ (accessed on 1 February 2018).

2   Robert D. Kaplan 'Burma: Where India and China Collide', in *Monsoon: The Indian Ocean and the Future of American Power*, (New York: Random House, 2011), pp. 213–39.

3   Ibid. p. 216.

America under President Trump appears to be going through an uncertain time. Under his 'America First' strategy, foreign policy is either handled clumsily, for example his recognition of Jerusalem as Israel's capital – a decision roundly condemned by the UN – or ignored altogether, and the Rohingya issue is probably yet to be added to his list of priorities. During Trump's address to the UN General Assembly in September 2017, at the height of the Rohingya ethnic cleansing, he failed to even mention their plight. Towards the end of November 2017, Secretary of State Rex Tillerson did criticise Myanmar, but while the US has always been enthusiastic about sanctioning countries for rights abuses, it is still quiet on Myanmar even though the world has recognised that the Rohingya are being treated inhumanely by their own government. Former US President Obama did see Myanmar's strategic importance within the lens of containing China as a rising superpower, but president Trump does not appear to have any interest in Myanmar, let alone sympathy for the poor Rohingya minority there.

China

As a neighbour and growing economic as well as political power in the world, China has a high stake in Myanmar and is conscious of the opportunities and challenges the latter brings. China needs to have a close relationship with Myanmar as it wants access to the Bay of Bengal and the Indian Ocean through Myanmar. Burma's deep-water ports, highways, and energy pipelines will 'provide China's landlocked south and west access to the sea'.[4]

China is also pragmatic enough to keep leverage over the anti-regime Burmese ethnic groups as well so that the Kachin, Wa and some other groups lean on China, and not on other countries, for any help. But when it comes to the Rohingya in Rakhine – their villages being burned to the ground and the community being uprooted from their homes – this probably does not mean much against China's long term economic interest in Myanmar. In the world of broken morality, the probability that the Rohingya are highly unlikely to return to Rakhine again may be considered as the more convenient option to both China and Myanmar.

The Myanmar leadership does not seem to be worried about international pressure to take back the Rohingya. It has its reliable

---

4   Ibid. p. 217.

friend with veto power in the UN Security Council, China, and in reality many Rohingya may not even be willing to return unless the UN and Myanmar government give them a cast-iron guarantee for their safety and the provision of basic necessities and rights. Myanmar has learnt how the American veto in the UN Security Council has allowed Israel to flout international law, *vis-à-vis* the Palestinians, for decades. The temptation for Myanmar is that it can do the same with China's help. Even if some Rohingya are allowed to return in any agreement, Myanmar can 'temporarily' house them in internment camps and procrastinate in rebuilding homes or shelter. The plain reality is that without the Myanmar government's genuine good will and material support, Rohingya homes simply will not be built! Myanmar's civilian–military government is fully aware that the already tired world community, or the chaotic Muslim world, will not be persistent enough to help the Rohingya or be generous enough to help in rebuilding their homes. The UN has stated that the Rohingya cannot be repatriated back to Myanmar against their wishes. The reality is the UN does not seem to have the appetite to assertively push the Rohingya agenda; it does not have the wherewithal to help these beleaguered people.

The China–Myanmar relationship, particularly post-Second World War, is based on mutual interest and as such there were bumps in the road of bilateral trade and investment.[5] Myanmar herself cannot satisfy China's hunger for energy, as it is not a hydrocarbon-rich country, but it is vitally important to China's land link with the Indian Ocean. China's strategic interest in Rakhine, on the coast of Bay of Bengal to the east of the Indian Ocean, is huge. In May 2017, it made a heavy infrastructure investment covering 4,000 acres at the Kyaukphyu port of Rakhine State as part of its 'One Belt, One Road' (OBOR) initiative that would allow it to hold a 70–85 per cent stake. Myanmar signed an agreement with China for a crude oil pipeline between Rakhine's Sittwe and Southern China's Kunming. This is part of a US$10 billion Kyaukphyu Special Economic Zone (SEZ) and is a huge undertaking, technologically and politically. A 2,400 km pipeline was opened on 29 January 2017 with little fanfare.[6]

---

5   Daniel Wagner, 'Energising China-Myanmar Relations' (*The Diplomatist*, March 2015). Available at: http://www.diplomatist.com/dipo201503/article013. html# (accessed on 1 February 2018).

6   Eric Meyer, 'With Oil and Gas Pipelines, China Takes A Shortcut through Myanmar' (*Forbes*, 9 February 2015). Available at: https://www.forbes.com/sites/ericrmeyer/2015/02/09/oil-and-gas-china-takes-a-shortcut/#300006df7aff (accessed on 1 February 2018).

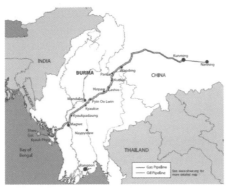

China's Kunming - Kyauk Phyu oil pipeline

Chinese enterprises, mostly state-owned, have been key developers in Myanmar for years. In the past, most of China's investments in Myanmar have been outside Rakhine State, but these current investments are new and very ambitious in projecting Chinese power in the region. The Kyaukphyu SEZ is China's dream project, which will give it access to the Indian Ocean and to the Middle East; China's hunger for energy needs direct access to Middle Eastern crude oil. This fits with its global aspirations of internationalising the economy. As an important part of China's trillion dollar OBOR initiative, this will give China a major foothold in the Bay of Bengal.

The unsympathetic role of China, Myanmar's key and powerful ally, to the plight of the Rohingya has been criticised widely. As the Myanmar government and military deny charges of ethnic cleansing of the Rohingya and refuse to cooperate with a UN fact-finding mission, China continues to provide it with diplomatic protection. In March 2017, 'China, backed by Russia, blocked a short UN Security Council statement on Myanmar'.[7] In September 2017, China 'resisted stronger involvement by the UN Security Council in addressing Myanmar's crisis'.[8] Although the Security Council unanimously expressed grave

7   Reuters Staff, 'China, Russia block U.N. council concern about Myanmar violence' (Reuters, 17 March 2017). Available at: https://www.reuters.com/article/us-myanmar-rohingya-un/china-russia-block-u-n-council-concern-about-myanmar-violence-idUSKBN16O2J6 (accessed on 1 February 2018).

8   News Desk, 'Analysis: China Backs Myanmar at UN Security Council' (*The Irrawaddy*, 1 September 2017). Available at: https://www.irrawaddy.com/news/burma/analysis-china-backs-myanmar-un-security-council.html (accessed on 1 February 2018).

concern over human rights violations by the Myanmar security forces against the Rohingya – such as killing, sexual violence and the burning of homes and property – China watered down the text by threatening to use its veto.

Nobody expects a global power to act for purely altruistic reasons, but China's role in the Rohingya crisis is being observed, as it could actually help a minority in Myanmar with its huge leverage on the country. Political observers are worried that long term instability in Rakhine can negatively affect not only Bangladesh but China and other Association of Southeast Asian Nations (ASEAN) countries in many ways. By being economically more prudent and politically long-sighted, China can help avert an unforeseen flashpoint which the Rohingya crisis might generate in the region in the future. Unless redressed with basic fairness and justice, a protracted and grave injustice against a people will inevitably bring chaos in the end. Given its huge investment in Myanmar's warm water, China needs a stable Rakhine. And there cannot be a stable Rakhine if the million-plus Rohingya remain homeless and rootless. Political stability and economic prosperity go hand in hand. China is in a better position to be an honest broker in this saga and pre-empt other envious powers who want to poke their nose into its southern border. It can initiate diplomatic efforts to resolve the Rohingya crisis involving Myanmar and Bangladesh before instability and security issues incentivise other non-government players as well.

India

China's enterprise southward and India's ambition eastward (to counter China) mean both powers have a great interest in Myanmar. China desperately needs Myanmar and India cannot afford to lose it either. India is also planning to build its own energy pipeline network through Myanmar, and this pipeline diplomacy in Rakhine State, between China and India, is part of the broader China–India relations.[9] Myanmar is aware this will bring the prosperity they need through employment, transit fees, and oil and gas revenues. This

9   Giuseppe Forino, Jason von Meding, and Thomas Johnson, 'The oil economics and land-grab politics behind Myanmar's Rohingya refugee crisis' (Quartz India, 12 September 2017). Available at: https://qz.com/1074906/rohingya-the-oil-economics-and-land-grab-politics-behind-myanmars-refugee-crisis/ (accessed on 1 February 2018).

competition for power and influence can make Myanmar a 'quiet strategic battleground', according to Kaplan.[10] However, Myanmar should not forget there are dangers as well. Aspiring global powers only care about their own interests!

The Rohingya catastrophe should thus be seen in the context of a rapidly evolving geo-political environment.[11] The Myanmar military probably feels it could withstand a tarnished international image without incurring sanctions. In spite of sustained discrimination and persecution of the Rohingya since the 1960s, the Myanmar military have got away with it. Their violent and savage treatment of the Rohingya and other ethnic groups has so far failed to result in any penalty from the UN or any other global power. On the contrary, rather than being punished it was rewarded by the US with the lifting of sanctions in October 2016 and has received significant help from the West in the form of aid, investment and trade. Even during the latest routing of the Rohingya, Myanmar received unequivocal support from China, Russia and India.

China and India are investing heavily for their own regional and geo-political interests, which has emboldened the generals and assured Suu Kyi that the UN and global frustration and anger will wither away in due course. It is true that major world powers have geo-political considerations that cannot be ignored in our real world, but when a minority is being treated savagely and exterminated by a country's military they cannot simply close their eyes or connive with the powerful. A world order based on the law of the jungle is dangerous for all. Genocides in Rwanda and Srebrenica a quarter of a century ago should not be so easily forgotten.

10   Kaplan, *Monsoon*, n. p.
11   Matteo Fumagalli, 'How geopolitics helped create the latest Rohingya crisis'(TheConversation,21 September2017).Availableat:https://theconversation. com/how-geopolitics-helped-create-the-latest-rohingya-crisis-84309(accessed on 1 February 2018).

8 Other Factors Impeding Justice for the Rohingya

The intractable Rohingya issue in Myanmar is tinged with complexity and it needs to be resolved with a multi-dimensional approach. The problems are not insurmountable but we have to realise that there are a number of factors, some historical, that need to be overcome. Key amongst them are:

(i) The legacy of a colonial policy, particularly during the Second World War.
(ii) The race to monopolise resources such as land, water, timber and precious stones.
(iii) The absence of Bangladesh's assertive diplomacy *vis-à-vis* Myanmar.
(iv) The weak role of ASEAN and other nations and agencies.

(i) The legacy of a colonial policy, particularly during the Second World War

We have to realise that the seeds of future problems were sown during British colonialism, particularly after the Japanese invasion of Burma during the Second World War. Buddhists supported Japan's occupation army, while the British needed support for their war effort, which they received from the Rohingya. Colonial powers like Britain made effective use of a 'divide and rule' policy – favouring one group over another for their own profit. In Arakan the Rohingya became the good guy for a while, but the ensuing division this created in Arakan, between the two main communities – the Rakhine Buddhists and Rohingya Muslims – became long lasting. The colonial rulers' unwillingness or failure to build bridges between the two communities after the war and before handing over independence to Burmese leaders provoked a deep cultural crisis in the state. Britain did not care about its social implications, as it was not their land, they just left – as they did in some other places. The historic ethno-religious division in Rakhine was fully utilised by Myanmar's military rulers, who furthered it with systemic discrimination against the Rohingya for their own narrow political goal. Under the patronage of the military, blind Burmese nationalist anger in Rakhine fell solely on the Rohingya.

In post-independence Burma, decades of prejudice, demonization, discrimination and 'othering' filled the minds of the Rakhine Buddhist population and others in Myanmar with an undisguised hatred toward the Rohingya, and in some cases against Muslims. Many ordinary Myanmar Buddhists truly believe that their religion and culture is under threat from the Rohingya population, although common sense informs that they are a small minority and their social and political capital has already been reduced to insignificance. The generally Islamophobic global environment, especially in the aftermath of President Bush's 'war on terror', might have played some part in their Rohingya-phobia. Unless there is now a solid strategy and practical steps to reduce this blind hatred, a sustainable long term solution to the suffering of the Rohingya is a far cry.

Repatriation and reconciliation must start with the acceptance that the Rohingya, as a human community, deserve basic respect and their ethnicity and history are recognised. Myanmar's military establishment and many Buddhist nationalists, including monks, have been painstakingly trying to establish that the Rohingya are aliens or immigrants, not deserving any basic human rights. Their denial of Rohingya history is a cloak used to demonise them: 'The Bengalis were not taken into the country by Myanmar, but by the colonialists',[1] claimed Myanmar's current military chief, Min Aung Hlaing, while talking with US Ambassador Scot Alan Marciel in Yangon on 11 October 2017. This is a deliberately selective reading of history to

---

1   RFA's Myanmar Service and Richard Finney, '"Bengalis" Not Native to Myanmar, Country's Military Chief Says' (Radio Free Asia, 12 October 2017). Available at: http://www.rfa.org/english/news/myanmar/bengalis-10122017191 055.html (accessed on 1 February 2018).

perpetuate persecution and injustice on the Rohingya. A few days later, the British-based Arakan Rohingya National Organisation (ARNO) challenged this distortion of history in a press release by quoting Nobel Laureate Professor Amartya Sen who said, 'Rohingya did not come to Burma. But the Burma came to Rohingya'.[2]

Even if the military chief and the proponents of this theory are right, as European colonialists often shifted people from one part of their Empire to another and some Bengalis were indeed brought to Arakan for economic reasons during British rule, do the Rohingya deserve to be systematically persecuted and ethnically cleansed in this manner? All countries in the last few centuries have accepted the new post-colonial realities; why should Myanmar be an exception?

(ii)   The race to monopolise resources such as land, water, timber and precious stones

Buddhist-Muslim conflict over land and resources in what is now Rakhine state is not new. From the fifteenth to eighteenth centuries there were struggles between Muslim empires expanding from the west and the Buddhist Arakan kingdom of Mrauk-U, ending only when the area was conquered by the kingdom of Burma in 1785. However, it was British colonialism (1826–1948) that arguably sowed the most dangerous seeds for the blind hatred and crisis currently facing the Rohingya. Burma was ruled as part of the British Raj, enabling inward migration from the Indian subcontinent. The British encouraged Bengalis in particular to migrate to address labour shortages on agricultural plantations. In Akyab district (present-day Sittwe), for instance, the Muslim population increased during British rule. By then, ethnic Indians had acquired prominent positions across the Burmese economy, as skilled professionals, merchants and financiers – not just agrarian Coolies. During the 1930s economic crisis, many Buddhist farmers became indebted to Indian moneylenders but some defaulted, leading Indians to become major landlords as well.

Economic nationalism, not dissimilar to racial or religious chauvinism, grew. It was not until Britain's defeat by invading Japanese forces in 1942 that communal violence erupted there. Rohingya Muslims were viewed with suspicion for their support of the British during the war. This intensified Buddhist nationalist feelings

---

2   Press release, 'How Long You Lie To Deny Rohingya Existence' (Burma Link, 15 October 2017). Available at: https://www.burmalink.org/how-long-you-lie-to-deny-rohingya-existence/ (accessed on 1 February 2018).

and a damaging legacy of this war-related unrest and displacement of people on both sides is that the Rohingya were gradually being depicted by nationalist Buddhists as 'illegal Bengali immigrants'. This unhappy development is what lies behind the subsequent rejection of the Rohingya as aliens by the Burmese military and chauvinist Buddhists. Decades of government propaganda, discriminatory educational provision, and anti-Rohingya narrative from Buddhist monks, some of whom subscribed to contagious Islamophobia, have created a paranoia against the Rohingya.

Rakhine state is Myanmar's second poorest region, although it is a resource-rich state. Development there has been slow with little local employment, as benefits are being monopolised by the regime and foreign investors. Religion and ethnicity are another important factor and persecution of the Rohingya in Myanmar in post-independence Burma has dominated the local and international news coverage, particularly in recent times. But this is not everything, ordinary Buddhists there are also struggling economically. While religion and ethnicity are major factors behind this brutal treatment of Rohingya people, the economic factor might have played an important part as well, as nationalist Buddhists blame their own economic misfortune on the Rohingya population. While state-led persecution of Burma's Muslim minority is worsening,[3] the treatment of the Rohingya is beyond the pale.

Economic profit was, of course, the main driver behind the European colonisation project. In the last few decades the world has seen a sharp rise in corporate greed by shareholders of multinationals or large companies. In Myanmar, and Rakhine in particular, acquisition of land for mining, timber, agriculture and water has become a big issue in recent years. The military itself was already taking land from Buddhist and other groups in the 1990s for 'development' projects, including military base expansions, natural resource exploitation and extraction, large agriculture projects, infrastructure and for tourism. For example, in Kachin state, the military confiscated more than 500 acres of villagers' land to support extensive gold mining.[4]

---

3   Press Release, 'Burma Human Rights Network publishes research revealing state-led persecution of Burma's Muslim minority' (BHRN, 5 September 2017). Available at: http://www.bhrn.org.uk/en/press-release/23-burma-human-rights-network-publishes-research-revealing-state-led-persecution-of-burma%E2%80%99s-muslim-minority.html (accessed on 1 February 2018).

4   Forino, von Meding and Johnson, 'The oil economics and land-grab politics behind Myanmar's Rohingya refugee crisis'.

Since 2012, in the aftermath of the Myanmar parliament's approval of land laws such as the Farmland Law and the Vacant Land Law that allowed 100 per cent foreign capital with lease periods of up to 70 years, foreign investors are taking massive advantage of the Myanmar economy. According to transparency campaigners Global Witness, jade stone mining alone generated almost US$31 billion from Burmese mines in 2014. 'Jade mining companies connected to the army in Myanmar may have carried out the biggest natural resources heist in modern history',[5] it claimed.

From a perversely selfish economic point of view, some suggest that the expulsion of the Rohingya 'others' makes sense; it serves the purpose of freeing up resources for economic exploitation. This may have a side benefit for the military, but it is not the main one behind their attempt to erase the Rohingya community.

(iii)   The absence of Bangladesh's assertive diplomacy *vis-à-vis* Myanmar

Bangladesh now finds itself between a rock and a hard place. Having given shelter to more than a million refugees and with little prospect of them returning home in the foreseeable future, Dhaka is bearing the brunt of unforeseen consequences.

The Rohingya crisis, essentially a situation for Myanmar to resolve, is affecting Bangladesh in many ways. Conversely, Bangladesh's role as a neighbouring country will impact on Rohingya ethnic cleansing and genocide in Myanmar. However, for decades Bangladesh's diplomatic weakness has been apparent. Bangladesh is geographically smaller than Myanmar, though with a much higher population (Myanmar's 53 million compared to Bangladesh's 160 million), so it has relative advantages and disadvantages. Nobody expects Bangladesh to be able to project its influence beyond its ability, but every country has a stake on what happens across its border.

The crisis has affected Bangladesh since at least 1978, when the first massive refugee influx from Rakhine entered the country. Just over a decade later, in 1990–91, there was another big wave of Rohingya refugees coming to Bangladesh. With the UN's help, Bangladesh somehow managed to return some of them, but the Bangladeshi government should have taken the Rohingya issue much

---

5   Jonah Fisher, 'Myanmar elite "profits from $31bn jade trade"' (BBC News, 23 October 2015). Available at: http://www.bbc.co.uk/news/world-asia-34600551 (accessed on 1 February 2018).

more seriously with Myanmar during the 1970s, 1980s and 1990s, either through bilateral diplomacy or through the UN. But as far as my knowledge goes, it remained passive all along and was not proactive in solving the crisis once and for all.

It showed a similar level of ineptitude, or even worse, in 2012 when tens of thousands of Rohingya again fled to Bangladesh. Life for the Rohingya has been made intolerable ever since. With over a million people now in slum-like refugee camps, Bangladesh cannot sustain the pressure for long unless the Rohingya are safely repatriated or taken to a place where they can live with better amenities and the provisions for educational development of their children. Bangladesh does not have a strong economic and social infrastructure and the long term stay of Rohingya refugees may have adverse social and political consequences in the future. With a fragile democracy under an overbearing government and the resulting absence of an effective political opposition, as well as the absence of a robust civil society to take the government to task, Bangladesh will be adversely affected as time goes by.

The Rohingya crisis has exposed serious weaknesses in Bangladesh's diplomatic capability as well. Although genuinely praised for its generosity, no permanent member of the UN Security Council has yet strongly backed Dhaka to solve the refugee problem. China put its weight behind Myanmar at the UN, so that it does not face any immediate threat of sanction from the West, but Bangladesh cannot even count on support from its closest ally and biggest neighbour, India. The Indian government's long term economic interest in Rakhine and Prime Minister Narendra Modi's known history of aversion for Muslims may be factors.

Bangladesh also has a strategically important geographic location, and with long term vision and political inclusivism its human resources can be transformed into a national asset; but this is missing. Given the size of its domestic market, it can be made more attractive to regional countries. Both China and India recognise this, and China decided to invest in Bangladesh as part of its OBOR mega project. Bangladeshi and Chinese firms signed trade and investment deals worth US$13.6 billion on the side-lines of President Xi Jinping's brief tour to Dhaka.[6]

---

6   Agence France-Presse, 'Bangladeshi and Chinese firms ink deals worth US$13.6 billion' (*Asia Times*, 14 October 2016). Available at: http://www.atimes.com/article/china-sign-record-us25-billion-loans-bangladesh/ (accessed on 1 February 2018).

This is in addition to US$20 billion in loan agreements that the two governments subsequently signed in October 2016. However, due to a lack of political vision and economic dynamism, Bangladesh's current trade and economy are apparently unable to compete with that of Myanmar. The latter has attracted massive investment from China, now an economic superpower awash with money. Myanmar appears to be more dynamic in projecting its advantages and getting more attention from the international community. Both Beijing and New Delhi are developing Myanmar's ports, including a deep-sea port, and Special Economic Zones (SEZ) in Rakhine. It appears to be better equipped at milking global investment as well.

Bangladesh has not so far strategically utilised its geography[7] and it has placed too much reliance on India, which has impeded its progress. This has not helped its image abroad and has also impeded confidence in its people. In recent years, not only Myanmar but even the small island-country of Sri Lanka has developed sophisticated maritime infrastructures including a deep-sea port. In the post-American South Asia, China and India have emerged as both economic partners and geo-political competitors. Rakhine, bordering with Bangladesh, is fast becoming an economic and geo-strategic hotspot on the Bay of Bengal. This offers both challenges and opportunities for Bangladesh.

If Bangladesh intends to be an influential economic and geo-political player in the Bay of Bengal, it must be proactive in regional and international diplomacy and maintain a clear balance between China and India. It also has no alternative but to develop a maritime infrastructure in Chittagong and a deep-sea port (Port of Payra) in Patuakhali, which was established by an Act of Parliament in 2013 and officially inaugurated in 2016. It is high time for Bangladesh to develop its economy by capitalising on the opportunities arising from China's Maritime Silk Road and taking advantage of its good relations with India. Bangladesh has a rich 4,000 year history and it needs to wake up, rise above its insularity and face its challenges, as well as grab opportunities, before Rakhine becomes the most important geo-economic hotspot. If Bangladesh fails in this then its port city of Chittagong will be impoverished and the country will remain dependent on regional powers.

---

7   M. Shahidul Islam, 'Bangladesh losing its geo-economic importance to Myanmar' (*The Daily Star*, 17 October 2017). Available at: http://www.thedailystar.net/opinion/economics/bangladesh-losing-its-geo-economic-importance-myanmar-1477267 (accessed on 1 February 2018).

(iv) The weak role of ASEAN and other nations and agencies

In the midst of the Rohingya expulsion to Bangladesh in August 2017, India's Prime Minister Modi flew straight to Naypyidaw from the BRICS Summit in China and gave Suu Kyi the support she desperately needed against international criticism for her silence. Modi comes from a Hindu nationalist background and his government even wanted to deport 40,000 Rohingya refugees, who took shelter in India after previous massacres, including 15,000 registered with the UNHCR. This provoked sharp criticism from the UN Human Rights Council.[8] India is apparently obsessed with reported links between the ARSA and transnational terror groups, which ARSA has categorically denied.

Nearly a dozen southeast Asian countries that formed the Association of Southeast Asian Nations (ASEAN) in 1967 – to promote Pan-Asianism and intergovernmental cooperation as well as facilitate better integration amongst its members and Asian states[9] – could have played a more dominant role in thwarting the Rohingya massacre. But it has failed dismally. While its foreign ministers issued a statement in September 2017 on the 'humanitarian situation in Rakhine State', this was foreshadowed by the ASEAN leaders' silence on the matter two months later, in its thirty-first summit in Manila on 10–14 November.[10] Its own Parliamentarians for Human Rights (APHR) said the failure 'constitutes a blow to the regional bloc's credibility'.[11] The final statement issued after the Southeast Asian summit made no mention of the exodus of Rohingya Muslims

---

8   TNN, 'UN rights body slams India for seeking deportation of Rohingyas' (*The Times of India*, 12 September 2017). Available at: https://timesofindia. indiatimes.com/india/un-rights-body-slams-india-for-seeking-deportation-of-rohingyas/articleshow/60470333.cms (accessed on 1 February 2018).

9   Chung-in Moon, 'ASEAN, international organization' (Encyclopædia Britannica, 20 July 1998). Available at: https://www.britannica.com/topic/ASEAN (accessed on 1 February 2018).

10   J.C. Gotinga, 'ASEAN summit silence on Rohingya "an absolute travesty"' (Al Jazeera, 14 November 2017). Available at: http://www.aljazeera.com/news/ 2017/11/asean-summit-silence-rohingya-absolute-travesty-171114211156144. html (accessed on 1 February 2018).

11   Press Release, 'ASEAN's failure to address drivers of Rohingya crisis undermines credibility, regional lawmakers warn' (ASEAN Parliamentarians for Human Rights, 15 November 2017). Available at: https://aseanmp.org/2017/11/15/ aseans-failure-to-address-drivers-of-rohingya-crisis-undermines-credibility-regional-lawmakers-warn/ (accessed on 1 February 2018).

from Myanmar's Rakhine state.[12] The role played so far by ASEAN's Muslim member countries on an issue that affects them, their neighbours as well as their co-religionists has been pathetic.

In the absence of American leadership, the EU, as a powerful economic bloc, could have played a significant role in not only alleviating Rohingya suffering through humanitarian aid, but also by pushing forward a sustainable peace plan through the UN. Europe should have been naturally empathic towards the Rohingya and come to their aid. Post-Holocaust Europe experienced another ethnic cleansing and genocide in Bosnia in the early 1990s, and with the help of America and NATO averted one in Kosovo in 1998–99, even without the approval of the UN Security Council.

The Rohingya crisis would not have come to this stage if the Organisation of Islamic Cooperation (OIC),[13] an international body consisting of fifty-seven member states and with a collective population of over 1.6 billion, was effective. Due to a lack of internal unity amongst member states and timidity in asserting its position, the OIC is punching under its weight in the international arena. The Rohingya are a Muslim minority and one of the main reasons for their suffering is their religious identity. East Timor was separated from Indonesia because the West had an interest in their co-religionists, the Christians. The West could do this because they had effective political, diplomatic and military power. The OIC leadership must ponder on their role.

At the end of the day, it is the UN which needs to be an effective arbiter amongst the member countries; else its relevance in the world will be further diminished. At the same time, the world community cannot afford to make the UN fail the way the League of Nations failed after the First World War and led to the global catastrophe in the form of the Second World War. What is needed is political will and diplomatic assertiveness from the UN leadership in order to bring the Security Council to a consensus to solve the humanitarian crisis and existential threat that the Rohingya are facing.

Although Britain is no longer a super power in terms of military and economic capability, it is still widely perceived as a diplomatic

---

12   Reuters Staff, 'Southeast Asia summit draft statement skips over Rohingya crisis' (Reuters, 13 November 2017). Available at: https://www.reuters.com/article/us-asean-summit-myanmar/southeast-asia-summit-draft-statement-skips-over-rohingya-crisis-idUSKBN1DD0CP?il=0 (accessed on 1 February 2018).

13   See, The Organization of Islamic Cooperation (https://www.oic-oci.org).

super power and has a moral obligation to come to the support of the beleaguered Rohingya people that once supported Britain and gave their blood to defeat the Japanese occupation of Burma in the Second World War. Britain has significant leverage on America, the EU and Commonwealth countries, including India. Although the Brexit negotiations have been keeping the government busy since 2016, Britain should use all its soft and silent power and meaningfully initiate a conversation with other permanent members of the UN Security Council and relevant important players to convince them of their moral obligation to help the Rohingya, or at least to not stand in the way of a just and sustainable solution to this man-made catastrophe.

9 What is to be done?

The UN was smartly sidestepped by Myanmar in its bid to solve the problems in Rakhine. Although the Advisory Commission on Rakhine State, chaired by former UN Secretary-General Kofi Annan, did not address many core issues *vis-à-vis* the Rohingya, some of its recommendations may be useful in bringing peace to Rakhine. But this can only be relevant once the Rohingya are back in Rakhine and the world community cannot rely on Myanmar's good will. The UN must immediately initiate a process to arrange a complete repatriation plan for all forcibly displaced Rohingya people back to their homes in Rakhine. They must be taken back with a full guarantee of their inalienable rights, including full citizenship. The Myanmar–Bangladesh bilateral deal[1] that was unexpectedly announced on 23 November 2017 is not yet transparent to the world community. Any solution that is not comprehensive and has anything other than the full involvement of the UN will fail. Everything must be conducted under an international legal binding in the form of a UN Security Council resolution on the Rohingya.

The integration of the Rohingya as full citizens will need a comprehensive socio-cultural and political strategy focused on reducing bigotry and building bridges between the two communities. There must also be guarantees for freedom of movement as well as access to education, health, political representation and justice as full

---

1   Oliver Holmes and agencies, 'Myanmar signs pact with Bangladesh over Rohingya repatriation' (*The Guardian*, 23 November 2017). Available at: https://www.theguardian.com/world/2017/nov/23/myanmar-signs-pact-with-bangladesh-over-rohingya-repatriation (accessed on 2 February 2018).

citizens of the country. Without a firm guarantee of the Rohingyas safe return and their resettlement, no one from the community would risk, or should be forced, to return to their burnt homes again. With basic goodwill from Myanmar and the weight of consensus from the UN, this is not difficult. Once repatriation starts, the UN must monitor the progress and make sure all parties comply with the agreement. Some recommendations of the Advisory Commission can then take effect.

The Advisory Commission on Rakhine State addressed multiple issues that have divided the communities for decades. On the complexity of the problem it said:

> Rakhine State represents a complex mixture of poverty, under-development, inter-communal tension, and political and economic marginalisation. Local communities harbour deep-rooted fears of the intentions of other groups, and trust in government institutions is limited. In particular, the Government's ability to provide services – including protection – to all communities has for long been wanting. The Commission recognizes the complex nature of the challenges in Rakhine, and the lack of instant solutions.[2]

At the same time, regarding the previous mindless ARSA attacks (before the August 2017 one) that provoked a brutal and highly disproportionate reaction from Myanmar, the Commission said: 'While Myanmar has every right to defend its own territory, a highly militarised response is unlikely to bring peace to the area. What is needed is a calibrated approach – one that combines political, developmental, security and human rights responses to ensure that violence does not escalate and inter-communal tensions are kept under control.'[3]

In conclusion, on implementation of the recommendations the Commission suggested:

> A ministerial-level appointment to be made with the sole function of coordinating policy on Rakhine State and ensuring the effective implementation of the Rakhine Advisory Commission's recommendations. [...] This one-year minister-level appointee should be supported by a permanent and well-staffed secretariat, which will be an integral part of the Central

---

2   Advisory Commission, *Towards a Peaceful, Fair and Prosperous Future for the People of Rakhine*, p. 14.

3   Ibid. p. 10.

Committee on Implementation of Peace and Development in Rakhine State and support its work.[4]

This sounds promising, but given the mistrust amongst the Rohingya for the military-backed Myanmar government, whoever is appointed must come under the UN monitoring framework.

For its part, Bangladesh should have mounted an effective diplomatic offensive in 1977, and again in 1982, when the new citizenship laws issued by the Burmese government prevented the Rohingya from obtaining citizenship and rendered them stateless ever since. As a neighbouring country that has also suffered from this saga, Bangladesh's voice is important in any negotiation on the Rohingya issue. Its Prime Minister, Sheikh Hasina, outlined her five-point proposal[5] at the UN General Assembly session in New York in September 2017. Dhaka should now raise its game and assertively call for a UN Security Council resolution on the full-scale safe return of all the Rohingya on its soil, with full rights, since their first eviction in 1978.

The sprawling refugee camps in Cox's Bazar

---

4   Ibid. pp. 62–63.
5   BSS, '5-point proposal could resolve Rohingya crisis: PM' (*The Daily Star*, 16 October 2017). Available at: http://www.thedailystar.net/rohingya-crisis/5-point-proposal-could-resolve-myanmar-rohingya-crisis-says-bangladesh-prime-minister-sheikh-hasina-1477306 (accessed on 2 February 2068). The Bangladesh PM's five-point proposal was: Myanmar must unconditionally and immediately stop the violence and the practice of ethnic cleansing in the Rakhine State; the UN

No sensible Rohingya wants to return to Rakhine without a guarantee of their safety and a dignified return as a human being. Some Rohingya who were interviewed in the refugee camps in Bangladesh said they would 'go back to their homes in Rakhine State if they were convinced it would be safe, their land was restored to them and ownership was guaranteed and they were given Myanmar citizenship.'[6] The Rohingya community has faced some horrific issues, as one refugee reported:

> no new mosques could be built for the last 20 years; they have not been able to pray in existing mosques for the last 5 years; even in a village with 100 Muslim families and 5 Buddhist families, the village leader always has to be Buddhist; children have not been able/allowed to go to school since Aug 25, 2017; married couples are not allowed to have more than two children; birth registration has not been done for the last few years.[7]

Nevertheless, one's motherland always has a magnetic attraction and for most Rohingya, Rackhine State is home.

The actions of the Myanmar regime in making the Rohingya stateless and driving them to Bangladesh are untenable and unacceptable, from a legal, moral and historical point of view. The planet earth can feed all of us if a tiny few are not too greedy. Myanmar is a sparsely populated country with a relatively large area; the country can afford to accommodate a small minority with a rich history who were caught up in the war between colonial Britain and invading Japan. There are human and positive ways of healing people's enmity. Myanmar needs a genuine reconciliation between people if it wants to become a successful country. The country's natural resources and geographical location can make it a rich country with the ability to

---

Secretary-General should immediately send a fact-finding mission to Myanmar; all civilians, irrespective of religion and ethnicity, must be protected in Myanmar. For that 'safe zones' could be created inside Myanmar under UN supervision; the sustainable return of all forcibly displaced Rohingyas in Bangladesh to their homes in Myanmar; the recommendations of Kofi Annan's Commission report must be immediately implemented unconditionally and in its entirety.

6   Julian Francis, 'Rohingyas: The unpredictable way forward' (bdnews24. com, 9 December 2017). Available at: https://opinion.bdnews24.com/2017/12/09/rohingyas-the-unpredictable-way-forward/ (accessed on 6 February 2018).

7   Ibid.

sustain its people, including the small Rohingya minority. With a new democratic approach, Myanmar can develop a more robust civil society, which as the eyes and ears of Myanmar can champion for a better democratic environment of freedom, openness and tolerance. Only through a culture of inclusivity can Myanmar's many diverse people live peacefully with one another again and rebuild the country.

Conclusion

The Rohingya people are enduring an existential crisis because of the hatred, discrimination and violence inflicted on them for decades that has culminated in Myanmar's ethnic cleansing and genocidal steps of uprooting them from their ancestral home. More than one million refugees, according to the most recent UN assessment, are living in dire and desperate conditions in Bangladesh, itself a poor nation. This is untenable in the long run, so nothing short of a comprehensive approach will be suitable for them. That means that in a short period of time Myanmar should take the Rohingya back, under the auspices of the UN, give them full citizenship status and respect their rights and dignity.

The Rohingya are the poorest of the poor, to the extent that most of the displaced people are not even seen to have their own mobile phones! Decades of prejudice, discrimination and persecution have rendered 80 per cent of the Rohingya illiterate, with 60 per cent of their children not being allowed to attend Rakhine schools – even though education is every child's basic right. High illiteracy, violence and economic deprivation have shattered their confidence and demolished their social capital.

But violence cannot be a remedy; more violence makes things worse and produces nihilistic groups hell-bent on extremism and terrorism. Rakhine needs a comprehensive solution with multi-dimensional approaches – immediate repatriation, humanitarian aid, and then socio-economic and political support in the process. Buddhists form a majority in Myanmar and if they truly follow the philosophy of Buddhism they are supposed to practice self-restraint against killing. But, like any other people, the perpetrators of these atrocities in Myanmar may have lost their religious spirit or may be using religion as a cloak to excuse their inhumane behaviour. Like other co-religionists, they should step back and think whether their religion teaches them to hate, discriminate, dehumanise and eliminate others.

Hatred and division can cause calamitous consequences for a group and should not be the fate of humanity. There are civilised ways of solving internal problems and creating a society based on universal human values of tolerance and respect. It is crucial to address the core issues that have divided the people in Rakhine. It is vital that Myanmar's civilian leadership find ways to reverse decades of discrimination against a small but historic minority which is now impoverished and dispossessed, and after the 2017 ethnic cleansing and genocide, completely pauperised. A military possesses weapons and thus wields massive power, so they should be under civilian authority to avoid its misuse. There must be a practical way, within Buddhist and Islamic traditions, of bringing people together. Pandering to military diktat is anything but moral, especially if it brings about the destruction of people and aversion from the international community. Suu Kyi can help in this solution if her 'democratic genes' override her nationalist tendency; democrats across the world will then feel empowered by her actions.

The world has seen enough violence and hatred in recent times, a situation that has forcibly displaced over 65 million people, nearly the size of Britain's population! There must be a human and political solution that takes into consideration the economic, ethno-religious and historical realities. The fate of Myanmar, Bangladesh and ASEAN countries are inextricably linked. Millions of people in the region live below poverty levels or are struggling to survive. Political leadership in Myanmar, in the region and across the globe have an obligation to find a lasting solution in Rakhine. It will be highly unethical and imprudent for global and regional powers or stakeholders to put their political, economic or so-called 'national interest' above the lives of a people.

The Rohingya deserve not just subsistence and mercy to keep on going; they need the capacity and confidence to rebuild their lives. Until their repatriation as a minority in their own land is guaranteed, the Rohingya refugees need child-friendly spaces, where their children can grow up in a safe and caring environment and they can play, read, feel loved and be educated. All of the humanitarian agencies working in the refugee camps must place special care on this as the Rohingya children are the future of their nation. The Rohingya people are at the crossroads of their physical existence, as is the international community in their moral, ethical and legal obligation to support them. Let us all work together positively, passionately and decisively towards finding the just and sustainable solution that the Rohingya are craving for.

Global situations change; history is cyclical. No country and human group should think it is above the law and lose its sense of obligation to others. There are challenges in any human society; resources are limited, but human greed is not. There are bad apples everywhere, no community has the monopoly in being rotten. Buddhists were known to be a non-violent people, but in Rakhine Myanmar Buddhists have thus far proved otherwise! If the Rohingya crisis is not resolved soon, it may haunt the whole of Myanmar and the entire southeast Asian region.

Some say our world today is going through a degradation of human, moral and ethical standards for which there will be a huge, tragic price to pay in the future. Others compare the current situation as no different to what happened during the 1930s, when Europe was sleepwalking towards an unknown catastrophe – death, destruction and holocaust. The whole world paid dearly for the early silence of those who could have averted this. Current global powers may be busy with a 'cost–benefit analysis' of their 'national interest' in world crises, but if they remain silent for too long history will judge them as complicit. Resolving humanitarian crises is the moral responsibility of the world community; the UN was tasked to do this after the horrors of the Second World War. If it keeps on failing, the world's moral order will be severely weakened, which could usher in a catastrophe for all!

The world community and the UN should quickly assess the horrible persecution of the minority Rohingya in all areas of life. Genocide or ethnic cleansing – whatever the terminology – will mean nothing to the Rohingya until the world says 'enough is enough' and comes to their protection, ensuring repatriation with basic rights and dignity as fellow human beings. As the British prime minister said in November 2017, we must do 'everything possible to stop this appalling and inhuman destruction of the Rohingya people'.[1]

If this ethnic cleansing, destruction or genocidal treatment of Rohingyas does not evoke global anger and a practical action plan to find a solution, particularly from the UN Security Council, then the world may one day succumb to the 'law of the jungle' that could unleash a 'might is right' form of violence by the powerful against the weak, to everyone's peril.

Facing a crisis is the time a nation decides either to give up or rise up. As a nation, the Rohingya are suffering a hellish existence – totally isolated, in IDP or refugee camps and elsewhere – and they can either become fatalists and give up on their future or stand up and be counted. With almost no alternative source of income, most Rohingya see no hope and in such desperate situations some criminal elements, some

---

1   May, 'PM speech to the Lord Mayor's Banquet 2017'.

Refugees at Cox's Bazar

even from within the Rohingya community, may resort to heinous acts of crime, participating in the sex trade or human trafficking! The UN has already warned about this[2] and it must not be allowed to happen.

The Rohingya have no other option but to invest in building themselves, their children and their future. An educated and self-reliant people can never be permanently subdued. The Rohingya had a thriving past, not because they were a big empire but because they nurtured knowledge, acted on it and built a successful and diverse society with their hard work. In the current situation this may sound nostalgic, but a people that aim for dignity can build their future. The Rohingya simply have to practise the best of their religious tradition that many within them might have forgotten and act with courage and determination. It is time they regain full confidence in themselves and reclaim the timeless lesson from their religious text: '*God will not change the condition of a people until they change what is in themselves.*'[3]

---

2   News Desk, 'UN warns of trafficking, sexual abuse in shadow of Rohingya refugee crisis' (UN News Centre, 14 November 2017). Available at: http://www.un.org/apps/news/story.asp?NewsID=58082#.Wki1-d9l_IV (accessed on 2 February 2018).

3   The Qur'an (*al-Ra'd* 13: 11).

The diaspora Rohingya, wherever they are, have a particular task ahead of them. From their position of relative stability they should rise to the challenges of time, try to rebuild themselves and offer their selfless services to the rest of their nation by investing in education, enterprise and skills. The diaspora Bangladeshi who have already established themselves as a successful community, particularly in some western countries, have their share of obligations towards helping the fellow Rohingya people.

The Rohingya people may be dispossessed and impoverished at this moment in history, but it is hoped that one day they will rise up with all the qualities that made them great in the past.

Index